DAILY WORD for COUPLES

Enriching Our Love in a Relationship of Heart and Soul

Written and edited by Colleen Zuck,
Janie Wright, and Elaine Meyer

Daybreak® Books
An Imprint of Rodale Books

Daybreak is a registered trademark of Rodale Inc.

Printed in the United States of America
Rodale Inc. makes every effort to use acid-free ∞, recycled paper ♻

Cover Designer: Joanna Williams
Cover Illustrator: Vicki Wehrman
Photographs are courtesy of the celebrities pictured.

Library of Congress Cataloging-in-Publication Data

Zuck, Colleen.
    Daily word for couples : enriching our love in a relationship of heart and soul / written and edited by Colleen Zuck, Janie Wright, and Elaine Meyer.
       p.   cm.
    ISBN 1–57954–215–8 hardcover
    1. Spouses—Prayer-books and devotions—English.
2. Devotional calendars.   I. Wright, Janie.   II. Meyer, Elaine.
III. Title.
BV4596.M3 Z83   2001
242'.644—dc21   00–066021

Distributed to the book trade by St. Martin's Press

2 4 6 8 10 9 7 5 3 1   hardcover

Visit us on the Web at www.rodalebooks.com, or call us toll-free at (800) 848-4735.

OUR PURPOSE

We publish books that empower people's minds and spirits.

An Invitation

Daily Word is the magazine of Silent Unity, a worldwide prayer ministry now in its second century of service. Silent Unity believes that:

◆ *All people are sacred*
◆ *God is present in all situations*
◆ *Everyone is worthy of love, peace, health, and prosperity*

Silent Unity prays with all who ask for prayer. Every prayer request is held in absolute confidence, and there is never a charge. You are invited to contact Silent Unity 24 hours a day, any day of the year.

Write: Silent Unity, 1901 NW Blue Parkway
Unity Village, MO 64065-0001
Or call: (816) 969-2000   Fax: (816) 251-3554
www.unityworldhq.org

There's More!

If you enjoy these inspirational messages, you may wish to subscribe to *Daily Word* magazine and receive a fresh, contemporary, uplifting message for each day of the month. With its inclusive, universal language, this pocket-size magazine is a friend to millions of people around the world.

For a free sample copy or for subscription information regarding *Daily Word* in English (regular and large-type editions) or in Spanish, please write:

Silent Unity, 1901 NW Blue Parkway
Unity Village, MO 64065-0001
Or call: (800) 669-0282   Fax: (816) 251-3554
www.unityworldhq.org

LIST OF ARTICLES

INTRODUCTION

A couple brings sacredness to their relationship by drawing upon the spirit of God within. As you and your partner do this, you follow a divine plan that has been unfolding throughout eternity, making and keeping a heart-and-soul connection with each other. Most likely, transforming your individual lives into a shared life has not always been easy. Such a commitment is a bond of a lifetime that encourages you to honor your love for and dedication to each other in the best of times and what may be perceived as the worst of times.

Daily Word for Couples was written for all the times of a couple's life—to be a helpful guide to individuals in sharing a life of love together. Reminded that God's spirit unites you, you are the loving, considerate people you want each other to be. Because you are, you bring out the best in each other.

Daily Word for Couples is about enriching your love for each other. You will, as never before, open yourselves to giving love and allowing yourselves to be loved. Most important, you will treat your relationship, your marriage, as the ever unfolding divine plan that it truly is.

You are God's love in expression in your relationship, and as you open your life together to the presence of God, you will discover the immense joy that an awareness of God within you and within each other brings to your marriage.

How to Use This Book

1. Articles: There are 11 inspiring stories written by individuals about their relationships, marriages, and families.

Dorothy Bridges, a recent widow, offers a no-nonsense friendly talk on the subject of marriage, giving insights from her 60-year marriage to actor Lloyd Bridges.

Both Jayne Meadows-Allen and Steve Allen, born halfway around the world from each other, tell of their early lives, of how they met by seeming chance, and of their commitment to love each other throughout 47 years of married life.

In an article by Roger Crawford, learn how a young man who may have seemed less than physically whole by some is loved and accepted by a woman who first befriends him and then becomes the love of his life, his wife.

2. Daily messages: Each spiritually enriching meditation is written in the voice of a loving couple. Read them together, to each other, or by yourself. They will direct you in being all that you truly desire to be. The affirmations are easy to remember so that you can affirm them throughout the day, and Bible verses are featured in support of the messages.

3. Our Prayer: Praying together is a sacred experience of uniting heart and soul that enriches a relationship. The prayers in this book are ones that will help you establish prayer times together. After reading a prayer, you may choose to simply be quiet and observe a few moments of silence together.

4. My Gift to You: You will be prompted to give a gift to each other after each prayer page. Giving the gift of your love, patience, or compassion for even 1 day will inspire you both to be givers and receivers of these and other qualities that add warmth and meaning to your life and your relationship.

Expressing the love of God that is within, you are fulfilling your part in a divine plan: You are not only in love with each other, but also you are being love for each other.

—The Editors

MARRIAGE

BY DOROTHY BRIDGES

Marriage! It's a big and important word. It's a wonderful and scary word. Marriage has been defined, interpreted, and examined through the centuries by experts in many cultures and fields, both religious and scientific.

I dare to speak on this vast subject when my main qualification is simply many years of living, which included 60 years of marriage to the same man, actor Lloyd Bridges. Mine is merely a friendly talk from someone who is fondly interested in the subject and whose thoughts are based on the experience of a long and successful marriage.

What happens when you think you have found that special someone with whom you want to share your life? How do you know it is the right person? What are the criteria of marriage that give us hope for a happy future?

In Meredith Wilson's *The Music Man*, there is a scene in which a mother scolds her daughter for not being able to find a suitable husband. The mother complains that her daughter is too fussy. She goes on to question what in the world her daughter wants in a man. In the song, "My White Knight," the daughter explains that she wants a man who loves her more than he loves himself and who loves "us" more than he loves her.

This concept of unifying love is crucial to any two people lasting as a couple. When the ceremony takes place, "you" and "me" become "us." The bonding doesn't happen automatically. If there is to be a lasting union, there must be an investment of thought and spiritual awareness.

It is very important that a couple approach marriage aware of the responsibility they are assuming, because it is easier to be in love than it is to be married. Love alone cannot be expected to overcome all the problems that will arise. The law of compensation is always at work; there will be blissful times and miserable times. When the deeper aspects of togetherness are nourished, however, a strength that perhaps was never before possible will develop.

For most, the marriage starts when the honeymoon is over. Reality sets in when we roll up our sleeves and take on one of the most important jobs of our life: making our marriage work. What rewarding, creative work that can be, providing we are willing to meet the challenges.

Who of us knows all the secret formulas, the tried-and-

2

DAILY WORD FOR COUPLES

true methods that will guarantee the best results? Do we find the answers in books, in friendly or professional advice? If we use a pragmatic approach, we agree that whatever works will do. Above all is our realization of how important it is that we nourish and preserve the solidarity that so affects our life and the welfare of our family.

Will there be challenges? We can count on that. They will come from every direction, no matter how much in love or how wealthy or successful or virtuous we are. The promises we make at the altar are not easy to keep over time. Questions over money, raising the children, and other family matters can be major battlegrounds.

After a time of living side by side, we may happen to discover that the ideal, almost-perfect person we married displays some defects. Hopefully, they are minor ones, and we learn to cope. If we are wise, we realize that we, too, are not perfect and will need to have our faults endured.

The challenges of relationships are everywhere before our eyes—the subject of novels and soap operas, comedy and tragedy. We hear about them long before we are married, and we pray that we never have to meet them.

What if we do? This is the time we need help, especially when, in spite of our hopes and hard work, we don't have solutions that will save our marriage. This is the time to be more aware of the great worth and importance of "us." Now is the time to heed that ever true admonition, "let go and let God."

It is through faith in God, in something intangible that is larger and stronger than our individual selves, that we can overcome doubts and fears. We can find hope again. It is possible to turn our despair into forgiveness and to re-create love where there seems to be little or none. Instead of allowing our marriage and our family life to crumble, we discover that we can build a stronger and more practical bond than we have ever before experienced.

Marriage is one of the most important investments we make in life, and it comes with a price. As individuals, we are no longer the center of our life. If we don't already have lots of patience and understanding, we must acquire or enhance these virtues. We have to have a strong sense of responsibility and a sense of humor.

What is the return on this investment? It can reward us with things that money can't buy: companionship, enduring love, and a partner and family to share the joys and trials that fill every life.

In my long marriage to Lloyd, I learned what worked and didn't work for us. Whenever I have been asked to explain how our love lasted so long, I offer my personal advice.

Let marriage be a top priority in your life but don't be heavy-handed about it. If you can achieve it, the light touch—the feeling of ease—will enhance your relationship. If you are suspicious, always looking for trouble, you will usually find it.

As your partnership in life gathers strength, you'll find that it is the seemingly small things you have done for each other that has strengthened the bond of your connections.

My love affair with Lloyd began in college when I received a valentine from this very attractive young man. I wrote one for him, and we continued to exchange valentines every year. This one proved how meaningful the little things meant to us:

> *A valentine is more to me*
> *Than just lacy frivolity,*
> *A satin heart, a tinseled sweet*
> *Are empty symbols, incomplete.*
> *A valentine is when you rise*
> *To hushaby the baby's cries.*
> *A valentine is when you phone,*
> *And just to say, "What's new at home?"*
> *A valentine is when you shout*
> *"Take off that apron, let's eat out!"*
> *A valentine is when we kiss,*
> *Or talk at home one hour unharried.*
> *My valentine I say is this,*
> *The great big joy of being married.*

I strongly recommend that you never neglect the spiritual side of your life together. Whatever your religious beliefs, use them to enrich and sustain your relationship. It isn't just about going through rituals; it's about living the precepts you have learned and passing them on to your children so that their lives will be enriched.

Every morning at the family breakfast table, Lloyd or I read *Daily Word* magazine to our three children, even if they didn't always seem to understand or be interested. We always found some inspiration or insight from the words, and we hoped that somehow, someday, they would too. How rewarding that many years later Beau, Jeff, and Lucinda are married, reading *Daily Word* to their children.

In times of greatest stress in our marriage, Lloyd and I tried to remember to let go and let God. Often after we had done our best to rectify mistakes we made and had just about given up trying to solve a problem, we put this spiritual principle to use. Then the miracle of understanding or reconciliation we needed took place, and our marriage survived.

I will give you a last bit of advice: If you are already married, enjoy it, nourish and preserve it if at all possible. If you're not married, don't be afraid. Try it; you'll like it!

I will leave you with one more poem—the one I wrote for Lloyd on our 60th and final anniversary:

Our prospects were unreal
But His loving strength was shown me
That day we bravely took
To the sea of matrimony.
Sharp reefs lay all around,
There was even distant thunder,
But we just set our sails
To be filled with love's new wonder.
How long the voyage has been
And how full of joy and laughter.
Some storms did come our way,
But there were always rainbows after.
The tide comes in, goes out,
Maybe sun and moon are paling,
But on our ship of love,
You'll find us sailing . . . sailing . . . sailing. . . .

Day 1

———◆———

*Together, we have made a lifetime commitment
to love and respect each other.*

**FINDING
EACH
OTHER**
We realize that our finding each
other was not by chance because
when we did, we united in heart and
soul. Perhaps before we met, our
prayers were the same: "God, help me to find the
person with whom a mutual lifetime commitment will
be made. In times of both abundance and need, we will
stay together and help each other."

What we have experienced together probably has
surpassed our expectations of what would be the easiest
and the most difficult. We are learning together and
growing together. Our choice is that whatever comes
our way, we will handle it together. We will because we
recognize that we are creations of God's life and love.

Because this sacred vision is our true picture of each
other and our relationship, it is always possible for us to
love and respect each other.

"Ask, and it will be given you; search, and you will find;
knock, and the door will be opened for you. For everyone
who asks receives, and everyone who searches finds, and
for everyone who knocks, the door will be opened."
—Matthew 7:7–8

Day 2

—◆—

*We give our very best by giving from
the spirit of God within us.*

**WHAT WE
HAVE
TO GIVE**

Asking ourselves, "What do I have
to give in a marriage?" gives us
incredible insight into the rewards of
offering our best to each other.

How can we make things better for us and between
us? At times, we may need to begin a conversation that
helps us understand what the other is thinking and
feeling. At other times, we may need to just be quiet
and pray that God will help us resolve something that
we are unable to resolve on our own.

When we are giving from the spirit of God at the
core of our beings, we are giving the very best we can
give. We have much to give to each other. In that
experience of giving, we allow the spirit of God to
move through our words and actions. We are helping to
create a bond in which giving the best is an everyday
occurrence for us.

"In all this I have given you an example . . . for he himself
said, 'It is more blessed to give than to receive.' "
—Acts 20:35

Day 3

—◆—

Speaking from the love of God within us,
you and I encourage each other.

ENCOURAGING WORDS Words are powerful; when spoken from the love of God within, they can build up a relationship. As you and I let the love of God express through us, we speak words that are loving, kind, and considerate.

Loving words encourage the one speaking them and encourage the one being spoken to. Encouraging words strengthen us as individuals and as a couple.

If we let emotions of hurt or disappointment speak through us, we say things we really don't mean. We will always mean what we say when we give voice to the child of God that is within us waiting to express encouragement.

Looking on the sunny side of our life together is not denying that there may be times when we will walk in the shadow. Yet the warmth of our words will comfort and inspire us as we continue on our path.

"Therefore encourage one another and build up
each other, as indeed you are doing."
—1 Thessalonians 5:11

Day 4

—◆—

*Our expectation is that God's blessings
will be revealed.*

EXPECTATIONS

Regardless of what we have planned for today, we will probably go into each experience with certain expectations.

We also have certain expectations of ourselves—how we will act or react to what is going on around us and the ways others will respond to us. Yet we know not to allow our own expectations limit what we are capable of achieving. God created us, and as God's creations, we are capable of achieving wonderful, unimaginable things.

So we remain calm when events do not occur exactly as we thought they would. We let God guide each event and remain ready to be blessed.

While we may surprise each other at times, we welcome each new experience and thank God for showing us a richer, more complete side of each other.

"They voluntarily gave according to their means,
and even beyond their means . . . and this, not merely
as we expected; they gave themselves first to the Lord."
—2 Corinthians 8:3, 5

Day 5

—◆—

*Our home is on the sacred ground
of God's presence.*

**OUR
HOME**

It takes more than walls and a roof
to make our home—for a home is a
place where love abides and where all
who enter feel love as a tangible,
soothing presence.

That kind of love is divine in nature, because it comes
from the spirit of God within us. It is by acknowledging
that the presence of God is everywhere that we make
our dwelling a home.

Peace is a direct result of God's spirit of love actively
at work in our lives and in our home. Where there are
peace and harmony, tension and stress cannot abide. As
family and friends enter our home and our life, the
comfort they feel will give them a sense of welcome
and love.

Our home is built on sacred ground and is blessed by
God's presence. We maintain our home with faith and
love. Yes, God helps us make our house a home.

"Above all, clothe yourselves with love, which binds
everything together in perfect harmony."
—Colossians 3:14

Day 6
—◆—

Because we are loving,
we are thoughtful and considerate.

THOUGHTFUL
Sharing our lives is something we do because it is a desire of our hearts. Being thoughtful and considerate comes naturally, because we always want to be a source of peace and love for each other. We love each other, and we let our consideration and respect show in all that we say and do for each other.

God guides us both in loving and treating each other the way we want to be loved and treated. When we say "Thank you" and "I love you" we are expressing our appreciation for all that we do for each other and with each other.

We do not judge or criticize as we voice our thoughts and feelings. Knowing the importance of sharing, we each are interested in what the other has to say. Extending our hearts in love, we live our life as loving companions.

"Let us choose what is right;
let us determine among ourselves what is good."
—Job 34:4

DAILY WORD FOR COUPLES

Day 7

—◆—

Mature in the wisdom and love of God, we make adjustments that enhance our relationship.

MAKING ADJUSTMENTS

An important part of the fulfillment we experience as a loving couple is learning about life with each other. Then *my* way of doing something and *your* way of doing something meld into *our* way of doing it. Or we respect each other's choice when our ways differ.

In a spirit of cooperation, we make adjustments in our goals and in our everyday activities. Insignificant matters will never grow into large obstacles when we are willing to make adjustments. We will not feel as if we are giving up our individual preferences when we know that we are shaping and molding something bigger—our relationship.

We are mature in the wisdom and love of God, which ensures that we are always saying and doing what enriches our relationship.

"Let endurance have its full effect, so that you may be mature and complete, lacking in nothing."
—James 1:4

Day 8

— ◆ —

As we truly listen, we hear what each other is saying and understand what each other is feeling.

LISTENING Communication includes both speaking and listening. To ensure that our lines of communication are open, there are times when the most important thing we can do is listen.

In order to be good listeners, we remain approachable at all times, so that we feel comfortable telling each other anything that is in our hearts or on our minds.

Giving our time and attention to each other is an expression of our mutual love. As we listen, we are encouraging each other to talk about our innermost thoughts and concerns. Listening with our entire focus, we hear what each other is saying and feeling. After listening attentively, we offer our support and encouragement. Our love for each other creates an atmosphere of trust, and we feel free to share anything and everything.

"Finally, all of you, have unity of spirit, sympathy, love for one another, a tender heart, and a humble mind. . . . It is for this that you were called—that you might inherit a blessing."—1 Peter 3:8–9

DAILY WORD FOR COUPLES

Day 9

◆

*We are partners in life
and in spirit.*

PARTNERSHIP There are those who probably never would have picked the two of us as having the potential to be a long-term couple, but we know that God did. It's amazing how the wonder of God moved through other people and events to bring us together at the right time and the right place. Yet beyond all that, something else was needed: We were willing to be partners.

We are partners in life and in spirit, complementing each other by contributing our individual strengths and talents to our relationship. We support each other by letting our spiritual natures be a part of all that we are and all that we share.

Ours is a partnership in which the love and caring we have for each other is written on our hearts and within our souls. We complete a circle of love that blesses us and blesses our family and friends.

"In him the whole structure is joined together and grows
into a holy temple in the Lord; in whom you also are built
together spiritually into a dwelling place for God."
—Ephesians 2:21–22

Day 10

—◆—

Our flexibility prepares us to receive both expected and unexpected blessings.

FLEXIBLE

Being flexible does not mean that we are giving in to the demands of one another. Rather, it means that we have open minds and hearts and that we are willing to consider the thoughts and opinions of others.

We can be flexible and still not forsake our own beliefs and opinions. In everyday communication between us, we allow flexibility to encourage harmony and clear communication. Our openness shows that we are willing to hear ideas that are new or different from our own.

Experiencing the freedom of allowing our lives to unfold according to God's plan, we do not become upset when changes or adjustments need to be made. Thankful that we are not limited by our own expectations, we are prepared to receive new and unexpected blessings.

> "The wisdom from above is first pure,
> then peaceable, gentle, willing to yield,
> full of mercy and good fruits."
> —James 3:17

Day 11

—◆—

God is in charge of our family.

GOD IS IN CHARGE — Throughout our lives, you and I will accept many responsibilities. However we accept those responsibilities—as companions, spouses, or parents—there is a way that will help us fulfill all our responsibilities. Living our lives as the children of God we were created to be, we are able to carry through with all our other responsibilities—to each other, to our family, and to our community.

For now and forever, God is in charge of our relationship and our family. We build a life together on this divine realization. In all matters great and small, God is with us to guide us as we share in making decisions that affect us and our whole family.

By turning to God in prayer and acting upon the guidance we receive, we are acknowledging that God is in charge. Filled with renewed strength of mind, we face each day with confidence.

> "I trust in the steadfast love of God
> forever and ever."
> —Psalms 52:8

Day 12

— ◆ —

*We are building our relationship
on the solid foundation of love, faith, and trust.*

SOLID FOUNDATION

Our relationship is a sacred union blessed by God. We love each other and accept each other as the unique individuals that we truly are. Building our relationship on the solid foundation of love, faith, and trust assures that we honor each other.

We love with an open heart and a dedication to giving the support and care we both need in times of crisis and during everyday challenges.

Having faith in God encourages us to have faith in ourselves as individuals and as helpmates to each other. We have been guided to share life's journey together, and our faith in each other builds with each passing year.

Because we both rely on divine guidance, we trust our own and each other's judgment. Together, we are building a relationship that will withstand the test of time.

"Father, I desire that those also, whom you have given me, may be with me where I am, to see my glory, which you have given me because you loved me before the foundation of the world."—John 17:24

Day 13

———◆———

*We are ready for each other because we are ready
to let God guide us in being loving companions.*

**READY
FOR EACH
OTHER**
I am ready for you and ready to be
your trusted, loving friend and
companion. I believe you are ready for
me also. We bring to our relationship a
commitment to recognize each other's needs and
respect each other's dreams.

We are open to letting the spirit of God answer every
question on our hearts and then prepared to follow the
guidance we receive.

All the years we have lived up to this moment and all
the experiences we have experienced have matured us,
but only God can prepare us to be a strong, united front
in the face of both adversity and opportunity.

Yes, we are ready for each other. I recognize the
presence of God in you, and you recognize the presence
of God in me. We are trusting, loving people who
delight in sharing life together.

> **"For everything there is a season, and a time
> for every matter under heaven."**
> **—Ecclesiastes 3:1**

Day 14

---◆---

Our Prayer

Dear God,

In our prayers to You today, we open our hearts and souls to the love You have for us and the love You have given us to share with each other.

We are so filled with Your love, God, that we understand how to be compassionate, true givers of support to each other and to our family and friends.

Thank You for showing us how to honor each other with our kindest thoughts, our most loving words, and our most helpful actions. We do value our union of love.

Reveal to us how we can continue to give blessings to each other, God, in all that we do. Through the wisdom You have given us, we are bringing an extra measure of harmony and love to each other and to every situation that we experience together.

> **"Open my eyes, so that I may behold wondrous things out of your law."**
> **—Psalms 119:18**

Day 15

—◆—

My Gift to You

I GIVE YOU THE GIFT OF MY COOPERATION.

I am giving you a gift today because I want to give you something of value, something that shows how much I love and appreciate you.

As I thought about what kind of gift to give you, all things made by human hands seemed inadequate. What seemed to convey my love and appreciation best was something that is as invisible as the wind itself but, like the wind, is a powerful force in life. It is my ability to cooperate, instilled within me by the Master Creator.

I am putting aside any tendency to disagree with you for 24 hours—at least. With an attitude based on believing in all that we can accomplish together, I am eager to share new experiences with you.

I give you my gift with no thought of what I may receive in return. I want you to know the joy I feel in giving my gift to you and in having you accept it.

"Now I appeal to you . . . that all of you be in agreement and that there be no divisions among you, but that you be united in the same mind and the same purpose."
—1 Corinthians 1:10

Day 16

———◆———

*Our relationship skills are words and actions
that have been inspired by God.*

**RELATIONSHIP
SKILLS**

The decision to share our life and love is one that our faith in God and confidence in each other led us to make. Our relationship is blessed as together and separately we turn to God for guidance in developing skills that enrich our relationship.

Such skills include knowing how to express love by word and action. We know how it feels when we tell each other "I love you!" We experience the joy of hearing those same heartfelt words spoken to us.

We are making progress every time we show respect for each other. We are making progress each time we care enough to listen to what the other is saying by putting aside the newspaper, telephone, or computer. Our relationship skills are simple. They include loving words and actions that have been inspired by God.

"But as for that in the good soil, these are
the ones who, when they hear the word, hold it fast
in an honest and good heart, and bear fruit
with patient endurance."
—Luke 8:15

Day 17

———◆———

*With faith in God, we move beyond past events
to the hope and love we now share.*

**MOVING
AHEAD**
Because we are creations of God's life and understanding, we have the capacity to love and to accept love. The love of God being expressed by us enables us to forgive completely and fully.

Whatever has happened between us or to either one of us individually needs to stay where it is—in the past. We move ahead as we turn to God in prayer. In a time of silent communion, God reminds us that past events cannot hurt us unless we continue to relive the memory of them.

Our faith in God bolsters our spirits so that we are encouraged about our relationship and how it can bring fulfillment to both of us—now and in the future. In God's presence, we can move beyond past events to the hope and love we now share. We can be at peace about the past and live at peace with each other in the present.

**"See, the former things have come to pass,
and new things I now declare."
—Isaiah 42:9**

Day 18

— ◆ —

Our loving hearts attract love back to us. Living in an atmosphere of love, our whole family is blessed.

LOVING HEARTS

The love and understanding between us are vital to our health and the health of our relationship.

Therefore we make sure that we give love and understanding to each other and to all the members of our family.

We bless and are blessed as we release the love in our hearts so that it moves out from us to enfold and fortify each other. Our love grows and expands to touch everyone in our family.

In this atmosphere of love, we are nourished and strengthened so that we have courage and live each day as it comes, no matter what may come. We know that with faith and love, we can overcome any obstacle.

United in love, our hearts lead us forward to share new adventures in life.

> **"God lives in us, and his love**
> **is perfected in us."**
> **—1 John 4:12**

Day 19

———◆———

We see each other clearly
as blessed children of God.

**CLEAR
VISION**

Time has and will continue to
change us both. Yet when we look at
ourselves in the mirror or at each other,
we see beyond our ever-changing
appearances. We see that we are eternally young in
spirit, for the spirit of God is within us.

We see God within as the spark of life that shines in
our eyes. No matter what changes time brings to us, we
will always love each other and recognize the beauty of
our inner spiritual natures.

Whenever we have a difference of opinion, we
appreciate that we can and do move beyond
temperament and ego by allowing the spirit of God to
express understanding through us. Our love is so strong
that disagreements cannot tear us apart.

With an inner vision, we see each other clearly—as
the one we love and also as the child of God that each
one of us truly is.

> "For now we see in a mirror, dimly, but then we
> will see face to face. Now I know only in part;
> then I will know fully."—1 Corinthians 13:12

Day 20

—◆—

Loving and being loved, we are filled
with a sense of wonder.

S E N S E
O F
W O N D E R

When our relationship was new, we were filled with hope for our dreams for the future. The life we live now may not be exactly what we had envisioned it would be, but we can still experience the sense of wonder that comes from loving each other.

Our love is true and pure, a gentle blessing of the uniting of our hearts that enriches our lives in wondrous ways. Nothing else may feel as joyous or as amazing to us as knowing that we love each other just as we are.

True love is an energy that permeates our lives. Although love cannot be measured in a standard way, it has the power to transform our lives. With a sense of wonder, we give thanks to God for the joy of loving and being loved.

"For surely I know the plans I have for you,
says the Lord, plans for your welfare and not for harm,
to give you a future with hope."
—Jeremiah 29:11

Day 21

—◆—

*As friends, caregivers, and confidantes, we are giving
something of value to each other.*

**OUR
ROLES**
As one-half of a sacred partnership
of love, we are each more than just an
individual. We are a spiritual whole
that includes each other.

We have many important roles to fill in our life
together, and we may fulfill several on any one day—as
friends, caregivers, and confidantes—yet always we are
dedicated to giving our love and support.

We honor our roles in our relationship and give
thanks for the loving support we receive in return. On
this most wondrous journey that is the unfoldment of
our life together, we are dedicated to being the best we
can be. By word and example, we encourage each other
and other family members to discover the joy of the
journey that each day brings.

In every role in which we give something of value,
we are sharing the blessings of God's everlasting love.

**"Some friends play at friendship but
a true friend sticks closer than one's nearest kin."
—Proverbs 18:24**

Day 22

God is our support system.

SUPPORT SYSTEM

We have the most powerful support system in all the world helping us in our union of love and life: God loves us and loves through us. God created us for life and wholeness.

As we invite the life and love of God to be expressed by us, we are supported in all that we do. Whenever we feel down, God will lift us up. Lifted up in spirit, we know the joy of God as we work together in making our relationship work.

Whenever one of us is challenged, the other is there to be the compassionate, loving helper. Nothing will get us down because God is constantly building us up.

We can always be a loving support to each other because God is the source of our life, love, and understanding. What a privilege it is to be supported by God in our union of love.

> "Remember that it is not you that support the root,
> but the root that supports you."
> **—Romans 11:18**

Day 23

———◆———

Together, we experience
the blessings of God.

**GOD IS
BLESSING
US**

There is surely no greater commitment than the one between two individuals who have dedicated themselves to loving and upholding each other for the rest of their lives. With their holy vows, two become one in mind, body, and spirit— dedicating themselves to loving and honoring each other for all the days of their lives.

This is a sacred commitment of the heart and soul that we share! What joy we feel in sharing new experiences that bring special meaning to our life. Through triumph and challenge, we are there for each other with a word of encouragement and a tender touch.

God is surely blessing us in mind, body, and spirit. With God as our guide, we care about and for each other and nurture our relationship for a lifetime.

> "They are no longer two, but one flesh.
> Therefore what God has joined together,
> let no one separate."
> —Matthew 19:6

Day 24

—◆—

*With willing hearts, we gladly do our part in making
our marriage one of shared blessings.*

OUR PART We want to keep our relationship
healthy and whole, so we know it is
important that we each do our part.
Whether we are taking care of
household chores or chaperoning our children on
school outings or providing part of our income, we
are dedicating our time and efforts to making our
marriage work.

Having a willing heart and a desire to make the most
of the sacred bond we share, we help keep our
relationship whole. If there are times when one of us
seems to be doing more, we know that an opportunity
for the other to contribute more will occur. What is
most important is that we are open to ways to help
each other and give our all in our relationship.

We know that it takes the love and dedication of
both of us to make our relationship work, and we are
both doing our part.

**"I am longing to see you so that I may share with you
some spiritual gift to strengthen you."
—Romans 1:11**

DAILY WORD FOR COUPLES

Day 25

◆

*Sowing seeds of kindness, we reap
a harvest of appreciation.*

**SEEDS
OF
KINDNESS**
An urge to give advice can be strong, bursting forth and sounding as if we are being critical rather than trying to be of help.

Perhaps the kindest thing we can do for each other at times is to not give advice. Instead, we silently pray that we find our own answers.

In sowing seeds of kindness, we help each other complete a project that is running late or one of us finishes a chore when the other is not feeling well.

We can also sow seeds of kindness by *not* doing anything: not pointing out what we perceive to be mistakes and not letting anyone or anything become more important than our being together.

Those seeds of kindness grow into a harvest of appreciation, because they are divine ideas that are given and blessed by God.

"Whoever pursues righteousness and kindness
will find life and honor."
—Proverbs 21:21

Day 26

———◆———

We are thinking of each other
and thanking God for each other.

THINKING OF EACH OTHER
What a blessing we share when we think the highest thoughts about each other. We think about each other when we pray, including each other in our prayers for health, peace of mind, and safety. We are always in each other's heart and on each other's mind.

Thinking of each other when we are together and when we are apart, we give thanks to God that we are a couple. Life would not be the same without each other. We feel such joy when we laugh together and such peace in quiet moments of knowing we are near to each other. As we express our mutual appreciation, it continues to grow.

During some very troubling times, we knew that we were praying for each other. Then, what we were facing didn't seem so much of a challenge.

Yes, we are thankful that God brought us together!

> "I thank my God every time I remember you,
> constantly praying with joy in every one
> of my prayers for all of you."
> —Philippians 1:3

Day 27

◆

*We honor our individual freedom of expression
by honoring each other's freedom to express.*

**FREEDOM
TO
EXPRESS**

A disagreement can have an emotional effect on both of us. Challenged by each other, we may begin to doubt our own judgment. Yet when we are able to take a step back from the situation and allow God's light to guide us, we begin to see that a disagreement is simply a difference of opinion, and that it is just one way to express our different views.

Our individual opinions are special to us, and we feel such freedom in being able to express them. We give each other that same freedom of expression. As we honor the wisdom within us, we are encouraging our faith and trust in each another and showing that we respect our diversity.

Because we are following God's guidance, we each know that our judgment will be sound and fair for everyone involved.

"Teach me good judgment and knowledge,
for I believe in your commandments."
—Psalms 119:66

Day 28

◆

*We are united by a promise to love each other
and to share our life together.*

**KEEPING
A
PROMISE**
In a union of our hearts, we are
making a sacred promise to share our
life together as a team. We entered into
this relationship because we love each
other, and over time, that love continues to grow and
bless us.

Just as the flame of a candle needs oxygen to burn,
our love needs our commitment of time and energy to
remain strong and shining brightly. God is with us to
uphold and guide us in keeping our sacred promise to
each other.

Love is patient and kind, and by remembering our
promise to love each other and to share our life together,
our relationship continues to blossom and grow.

You and I are united in a bond of love—with
ourselves and with God—and we are fulfilled by
sharing our life together.

"Do not neglect the gift that is in you. . . .
Put these things into practice, devote yourself to them,
so that all may see your progress."
—1 Timothy 4:14–15

Day 29

---◆---

Our Prayer

Dear God,

Thank You for bringing us together. Thank You also for continuing to bless us. Committed to doing all we can for each other, we share a life of love, joy, and happiness.

We do not take this commitment lightly, God, and we know that we can draw upon Your strength and wisdom at any time. We made a commitment when we spoke our vows, yet that was just the beginning of something wonderful. Our commitment continues with each loving word we speak, each thoughtful action we take. Without hesitation, we do what needs to be done to create and maintain an atmosphere of harmony and peace.

Thank You, God, for this blessed opportunity to share our faith and love as loving partners. We are committed to creating a lifetime of happy memories for us and for our entire family.

**"Commit your work to the Lord,
and your plans will be established."
—Proverbs 16:3**

Day 30

—◆—

My Gift to You

I GIVE YOU THE GIFT OF MY LOVE AND ACCEPTANCE.

Beloved, you are the joy of my life, and my gift to you today is the gift of my love and acceptance. Through every moment of this day, know that you can count on me.

I think of you enfolded in the love of God, and I see you as a beacon of that love for me and others. I pray that you are aware that as my love joins with yours, a stronger, greater love emerges.

Even when we are apart, I am sending my loving thoughts and prayers to you. I am envisioning you safe and secure and filled with the love of God wherever you go.

My prayer is that I will always listen to you with an open heart and mind, giving you the acceptance and understanding that enrich your life.

Now and throughout the day, I am praying for you and giving you the most precious gift that I could think to give you—the gift of my love and acceptance.

"Love one another."
—1 John 3:11

A COMMITMENT OF LOVE

BY JACK HANNA

As a longtime zoo director, I have discovered that the animal world offers us human beings so much to learn. Animals instinctively know to preserve their habitats and never waste food. They are dedicated to their families. Human parents can learn a lot from the way animal parents treat their young.

Marriage itself is a tremendous job, and raising children adds to a couple's responsibilities. Marriage and family, however, provide some of life's most tremendous rewards. As couples, we need to work at making our marriages work, and communication is an extremely important part of our working together. If both people play hardball and don't come to some kind of agreement that is acceptable to each one, then a little problem can build until it becomes a big problem—even over seemingly minor matters. Disagreements over money, a car, or a pet can break a couple apart. I know of one couple whose breakup began over the husband not taking out the garbage. They divorced!

My wife, Suzi, and I have been married for over 30 years. Like every couple going into a marriage, we didn't know what the outcome would be. Suzi and I attended the same college and at first became friends because of a pet donkey I brought with me. We both loved animals, and I would entertain Suzi with funny stories about the antics of my donkey. Still, I couldn't imagine this beautiful blonde cheerleader falling for a guy like me. I wore thick, Coke-bottle glasses and was no ladies' man. But one night we danced together, and that changed our relationship. We were married in our senior year.

Given enough time, the situations mentioned in the traditional wedding vows do come up for most couples—"for better, for worse, for richer, for poorer, in sickness and in health"—but it seems that fewer and fewer people are making the commitment "till death do us part."

We would all like to avoid being poor and sick, and often such challenges break up a family. When our 2-year-old daughter Julie was diagnosed with leukemia in 1976, married life was not easy for Suzi and me. We were living in Knoxville, Tennessee, at the time, and the doctors told us the best thing we could do for Julie was to take her 450 miles away to St. Jude Children's Research Hospital in Memphis.

DAILY WORD FOR COUPLES

While there, Julie was in isolation for 2 months. She received massive doses of radiation, chemotherapy, and bone marrow injections. During her time in isolation, we could only see Julie and talk to her through a glass window. We couldn't hold her or even touch her, but Suzi never left the hospital. We have two other daughters, Kathaleen and Suzanne, and I spent most of that time taking care of them back home in Knoxville.

We didn't think Julie would survive the first week in the hospital. In addition to leukemia, she also had a staph infection and pneumonia. Julie and another child were the only two out of twelve in the leukemia ward at that time who did survive.

Suzi and I relied on each other, the rest of our family and friends, and prayer to make it through. We were told that nearly 50 percent of couples with a critically ill child end up divorced. We knew we needed to be strong for our children and for each other.

When Julie finally did get out of isolation, we were so happy that we asked if we could take her back to our motel room for the night. What we really wanted to do was get away from the starkness of the hospital and how it reminded us of the illness. We hadn't gone far, though, when Julie became so sick to her stomach and so weak that we had to rush her back to the hospital. As much as we wished we could escape the illness and the side effects of her treatment, we could not. Thank God, Julie did recover and has been in remission from leukemia ever since.

In June of 1995, Julie was not feeling well and went to see our family doctor, who sent her to the hospital for a CAT scan and an MRI. These tests showed that Julie had a tumor the size of an orange in her brain. We were told that there were four other patients who as children had received the same treatment as Julie did at St. Jude's and later in life developed brain tumors—all were malignant. The high doses of radiation that had saved Julie as a child now seemed to threaten her life. When Julie's doctor talked to us after her surgery, he said, "Julie, your heavenly Father is looking after you—your tumor was benign."

I don't know that life in the Hanna family was ever normal. Kathaleen, Suzanne, and Julie grew up sharing their home with baby lions, a mynah bird, and other creatures. We had a zoo in our backyard—llama, deer, buffalo, elk, and chimpanzees, to name a few. The kids also shared their parents' love for animals. Kathaleen and I cohosted *Hanna's Ark*, my first TV show.

Suzi never complained, and as my career took off, she traveled with me all over the world, enduring the heat and primitive conditions of safari travel in India and Africa.

That's one of the rewards in a marriage: being able to do things together. Suzi loves the outdoors and animals, and I would not be where I am today if it were not for her. She has helped me raise animals and write my books, and she has been enthusiastic about everything I wanted to do. She is eager to get involved—from raising chimps to cleaning animal stalls.

Julie has a special gift for working with baby animals. She saved a snow leopard who was born with a caved-in chest by caring for him night and day for 6 months. Julie said that saving this baby from an endangered species was one way she could give back to life for her life being saved—twice!

Kathaleen lives in England with her husband, Julian, and is currently working on an animal television series of her own. I am very proud of Kathaleen and the fact that she is pursuing a career with wildlife. My daughter Suzanne lives in Cincinnati with her husband, Billy, daughter Brittany, and twins Alison and Blake, with one more child on the way. Suzanne's husband Billy is not only a great family man but also he's been involved with the Young Life organization for many years.

Having the same priorities and loving to do the same things have been important for Suzi and me, but our commitment to love one another and our commitment to work together have been essential to our staying together and raising our children. Life doesn't get much better than having the opportunity to watch the children you brought into the world grow up and thrive and have children of their own. And as Suzi and I grow older together, life just keeps getting better.

Day 31

—◆—

*From a starting point of declaring our love for each other,
we began a journey through life together.*

STARTING POINT Our journey through life began at an important starting point: It was a sacred time in which we declared our love for each other before God.

We have opened our lives to new experiences, from beginning a family of our own to maturing together as a couple. Every day of our journey, we can and do give expression to God's love.

We are living our promise to cherish the time that we have together by living in harmony with each other. We can because we have invited the spirit of God to live, think, and move through us.

From the starting point of our journey, we have worked together—each contributing our own unique personalities, experiences, and talents.

United by our faith in God and by our love of God, we live in spiritual oneness. We have come together and a wonderful journey is before us!

> "I will send down the showers in their season;
> they shall be showers of blessing."
> —Ezekiel 34:26

Day 32

---◆---

*Our conversations affirm the positive qualities
we bring to our life together.*

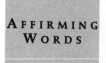
**AFFIRMING
WORDS**
Through the very words we speak
about and to each other, we are
helping each other. Whenever we are
speaking directly to each other or we
are speaking to someone else about each other, we
want our words to affirm the truth of who we are.

Whenever we are praying for each other, we give
thanks that we are creations of God who share a home
and family. Our prayers are affirmations about the
qualities we bring to our everyday life. We give thanks
that there are more of our qualities that are being
revealed as we continue to create a life together.

We are thankful that when we speak to or about each
other, we acknowledge our contribution to our
relationship. What a powerful revelation it is to be
aware of the good that God is expressing through us
and as us.

> "They shall speak of the glory of your kingdom,
> and tell of your power."
> —Psalms 145:11

Day 33

—◆—

*Working together, we shine the light of love
on all that we do with and for each other.*

**WORKING
TOGETHER**
Most projects and tasks go so much
more smoothly and quickly with two
people working together and sharing
the responsibilities.

We have noticed that this is true as we work around
our home. As we work together as a team, we get
things done quickly and efficiently. Because we are also
dedicated to sharing our lives together, we are dedicated
to sharing the work in keeping our home clean and
comfortable. Our love for each other is strong, and in all
areas of our relationship we are open to understanding
each other and sharing responsibilities.

Because our working together is about helping each
other, we don't keep score. Our caring attitude shines
the light of love on all that we do. We are sharing the
workload and also sharing the satisfaction of a home
that is maintained by love.

> **"Let us then pursue what makes for peace
> and for mutual upbuilding."**
> **—Romans 14:19**

Day 34

———◆———

Counting on God to help us be a loving, trusting couple,
we can count on each other.

**COUNTING
ON EACH
OTHER**

When we say, "You can count on
me!" we are reminding each other that
our happiness and well-being are
important to each of us. We can then
feel at peace when we are together and when we are
apart.

We may not always meet each other's or our own
expectations, but we understand that we are trying our
best. Our smiles convey encouragement, for it's as if we
are telling each other, "I appreciate the fact that you are
trying."

We are being wise when we let each other know
how much we appreciate some act of kindness or
consideration, for it encourages us to do more. Yes, we
can count on each other. Of even more importance,
we can count on God to help us be a loving, trusting
couple.

**"Therefore we ought to support such people,
so that we may become coworkers with the truth."
—3 John 1:8**

———————— 46 ————————

Day 35

—◆—

*We express our love for each other sincerely
and compassionately.*

EXPRESSING LOVE
Some people find it easier to express their love in words. Others are more comfortable expressing their feelings through loving actions.

We express our feelings for each other and our thoughts about life in our own unique ways, and that is okay, for we are unique creations of the Creator. What is far more important than the manner in which we express our feelings to one another is that we express them sincerely and compassionately.

While sharing our heartfelt feelings, we remember to give each other a chance to share. We do not respond without thought, but rather allow ourselves to absorb the significance of what the other has said or done. Then our responses are loving and kind, and our mutual trust continues to grow. With words and actions, we are telling each other and showing each other how loving and compassionate we can be.

**"How can we thank God enough for you in return for all the joy that we feel before our God because of you?"
—1 Thessalonians 3:9**

Day 36

◆

God is our solution.

OUR SOLUTION
If we have tried and tried to solve some problem and still the answer eludes us, it could be that we need to step away from the situation and pray about it. After spending time in communion with God, we return to the problem with a spiritually enriched perspective that leads us in finding the answer.

Problems may occur, but as we apply spiritual understanding to them, we will work them out together. With God to guide us, we will make the right decisions about our relationship and about all situations.

Divine order permeates our life. Trusting in God allows us to perceive that order. For every problem, God is the solution. And our faith assures us that God will never let us down.

"Go near, you yourself, and hear all that the Lord our God will say. Then tell us everything that the Lord our God tells you, and we will listen and do it."
—Deuteronomy 5:27

Day 37

— ◆ —

Recognizing the presence of God in each other,
we communicate in a language of the heart.

LANGUAGE OF THE HEART   There are many ways to communicate—with the spoken word, with body language, or through silence. No matter how we are expressing ourselves, we know that our desire is to always communicate in a language of the heart.

Because we acknowledge the presence of God within each of us and in our relationship, we find many ways to express our love. We remember those special times when we looked at each other and saw love shining forth from our eyes. What a sight that was!

When we have had a difficult day, we know that one of the best things we can do is to let our hearts speak through a hug of encouragement. Relaxing in each other's arms lets us know how right we are.

> "I will instruct you and teach you
> the way you should go."
> —Psalms 32:8

Day 38

—◆—

Being on time is one way we are considerate of each other.

ON TIME Our consideration for each other is vital to our relationship being a loving, long-lasting one. The little acts of consideration we show each other make such a positive and powerful difference. Even something as seemingly inconsequential as being on time is important.

If there is some event we are supposed to attend at a certain time or an appointment we have made, we allow ourselves plenty of time to get ready and still be on time. Being on time both individually and as a couple eliminates stress from our day.

We both know the importance of being prompt. It's just one more way of being thoughtful of and generous to each other. We are honoring each other by being considerate of our time.

> **"He has appointed a time for every matter, and for every work."**
> —Ecclesiastes 3:17

Day 39

— ◆ —

*We face each experience as the strong
and capable spiritual beings that we are.*

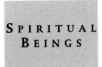
SPIRITUAL BEINGS Throughout life, there will be times when circumstances challenge us. During those times, we will discover strengths that we might never have realized we had.

Each experience is one in which we can learn more about our spiritual strength. Living from our spiritual nature, we understand that even though there seems to be disorder around us, we can remain grounded in the order of God.

Every day there is something to learn, and we know that we never need to shoulder any burden on our own because God's spirit enlivens us. We are spiritual beings who reflect our inner divine nature out into our life.

The spirit of God is at the core of our beings, so we know that we are strengthened by God. With this understanding, we have peace of mind.

> **"If there is a physical body,
> there is also a spiritual body."**
> **—1 Corinthians 15:44**

Day 40

---◆---

*In our dedication to serve God, we are fulfilled
in our work and bless others by what we do.*

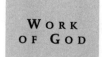

**WORK
OF GOD**

Like many people, we may spend a
large part of our waking hours at work,
so it is important that we like what we
do and feel that we are doing
something meaningful.

Whether we call what we do a job or a career, we
can and do dedicate it in service to God. In serving God,
we help others and are richly blessed ourselves.

And we pray to be understanding of how important
our respective work is—even when it seems as if one
of us is spending more time on the job and less time at
home. We take any concern to God and pray to be
understanding.

We may be guided to let go of concern or to talk with
each other about it. Or we may be led to simply honor
our different roles and give thanks that we are both
being fulfilled in what we do.

"We always give thanks to God for all of you
and mention you in our prayers, constantly remembering
before our God and Father your work of faith."
—1 Thessalonians 1:2

Day 41

---◆---

*Helping each other, we are in our right place,
doing the right thing.*

**LOVING
KINDNESS**
Love is powerful! Just a bit of our love expressed as kindness does so much to maintain the closeness between us. We enjoy thinking of ways we can make the day easier and more enjoyable for each other.

When we think about it, we know why we feel so good about being kind to each other: We are letting the love of God express through us as kind actions. How could we keep from feeling good about such a sacred activity!

Contrary to what it may seem at times, there is always enough time to be thoughtful. Only a few minutes of help by one of us can lighten the physical and emotional load of the other. When we see the tension on each other's face melt into a look of relief, we know that we are in our right place, doing the right thing.

"Love is patient; love is kind."
—1 Corinthians 13:4

Day 42

—◆—

*By honoring our parents, we are honoring
the family of God.*

**HONORING
PARENTS**

Honoring our own fathers and mothers is so integral to who we are. It is a sense of the importance of family that we apply in daily living.

Although getting along with family is not always easy, it is a desire of our hearts to honor the people through whom we made our entrance into the world and the other special people whom we call family.

The desire of our hearts is also to honor each other's mother and father with the same commitment to being kind and considerate. Having embraced each other, it's only natural that we embrace each other's whole family. Our parents hold a place of honor in each other's hearts.

Our family life is so much richer and fuller because we leave no one out.

"Honor your father and your mother,
so that your days may be long in the land that
the Lord your God is giving you."
—Exodus 20:12

Day 43

———◆———

*We are responsible for nurturing ourselves
and our relationship.*

RESPONSIBLE In any relationship, each person has responsibilities in making that relationship the very best it can be.

We have many responsibilities, but most important of all, we are responsible for ourselves. This responsibility includes finding fulfillment as individuals and as a team in our relationship with each other.

God gives us wisdom and strength so that we can do both. By relying on God, we are able to take care of ourselves and meet each other's needs. We are willing to be of help to others, yet we do not get caught up in doing for them what they can do for themselves. We allow time for maintaining our physical, mental, and spiritual well-being so that we can be a support to each other and our entire family.

> **"Take action, for it is your duty, and we
> are with you; be strong, and do it."**
> **—Ezra 10:4**

Day 44

—◆—

Our Prayer

Dear God,

Our family is our greatest treasure, and the well-being of each one in our family is always uppermost on our minds and in our prayers.

These precious ones are the sunshine that fills our days. Knowing that Your presence is with them is our comfort at all times.

We pray that all are healthy and fulfilled. Whatever outer conditions may affect our health, our faith in You assures us that Your healing spirit within us will heal us.

Your love for us and our family fills us with such joy. Thank You, God, for the blessing of our loved ones and for the joy of knowing that they are spiritually whole and filled with life.

Our family is peaceful and joy-filled because we are aware that Your loving presence is within us and within our home.

"Jesus turned, and seeing her he said, 'Take heart, daughter; your faith has made you well.' "
—Matthew 9:22

Day 45

—◆—

My Gift to You

I GIVE YOU THE GIFT OF COMPASSION.

My spirits soar when I give you the gift of my compassion, for I know that I am doing something that benefits us both. When I am kindhearted, I am blessed by the kind thoughts and words before they move out to you. What I am doing is giving from the goodness of God's spirit that is within me. Each time I am compassionate, I am allowing myself to be more aware of God.

My gift of compassion may take the form of a silent prayer for you when you are distressed, a word of encouragement when you seem down, or a warm embrace when you feel lonely.

There is a tenderness in compassion that soothes the one giving and the one receiving it. Caring about and for each other, we establish a connection of love and acceptance and then strengthen that connection by being compassionate with each other every day.

> "The Lord is good to all, and his compassion
> is over all that he has made."
> —Psalms 145:9

Day 46

—◆—

We are important to each other
and to God.

IMPORTANT TO EACH OTHER

As creations of God, we are needed and important in making our relationship stronger and the world a better place in which to live and grow.

God created us with a divine purpose in mind and a plan for fulfilling our purpose—as a couple, as parents, and friends. Whatever our roles may be—together and individually—we honor them and the ways we make them uniquely our own. As a couple and as individuals, we have something of value to contribute to our relationship and to the world.

We both are needed and important in our relationship, and because of that understanding, we remember to tell each other how much we care for and appreciate each other. We have been truly blessed by the wonderful opportunity of sharing a life together.

> **"You are greatly beloved. So consider**
> **the word and understand the vision."**
> **—Daniel 9:23**

Day 47

— ◆ —

*Our future is secure, for God
is inspiring us day by day.*

**THE
FUTURE**

A crystal ball does not contain the answer to what the future holds for us. And even if it did, would we want to know? The thrill of adventure for us lies not within the outcome, but within the journey that we will take along the way.

Neither one of us knows exactly what *will* happen in the future nor even what to expect *might* happen. So how can we plan for the future when we do not know what the future holds? We follow a divine plan of investing our faith in God.

God inspires us in being gentle and loving with each other. Each day of being inspired by God leads us to a harmonious future. Because we are giving and receiving the blessings of openness and honesty today, we are building a trust that will support us tomorrow and continue to support us all the days of our life.

> "Do not be afraid, little flock,
> for it is your Father's good pleasure
> to give you the kingdom."
> —Luke 12:32

Day 48

—◆—

Sharing our interests and our faith,
we enrich our lives.

SHARED INTERESTS
We open new worlds of interest to each other—giving each other a much richer view of life by sharing our visions of life.

For instance, we share a vision of a flower garden—first as a plan when we work with our hands and imagination planting seeds. Then, when a show of texture, color, and variety burst forth as flowers, we see our vision of beauty!

Watching and listening to each other, we share a passion for life. It's as if something palpable yet invisible has been passed between us when we share our interests in people, art, and nature.

One thing that we both share is our faith in God. How powerful our shared faith is. When either of us feels down, the other is there offering encouragement. Because we are two people united by faith, we are doubly blessed.

"Crispus, the official of the synagogue, became a believer in the Lord, together with all his household."
—Acts 18:8

Day 49

—◆—

*As a loving couple, we express
our love as forgiveness.*

FORGIVENESS With each act of forgiveness, we are offering a gift from the heart: The love in forgiveness helps us dissolve anything that would come between us and our living together in peace and harmony. With thoughts and words of forgiveness, we are agreeing not to keep reliving hurtful times in the past. We are agreeing to give ourselves a fresh start at being a loving couple.

Forgiving each other may not seem to be the easy response at the moment, but it does strengthen our union when it is both given and accepted with heartfelt sincerity.

We pray so that we both remain open to giving and receiving forgiveness. As we continue on in life, we are building on our trust in each other. Being kind and tender in all our interactions, we are fulfilled.

**"Be kind to one another, tenderhearted, forgiving one
another, as God in Christ has forgiven you."
—Ephesians 4:32**

Day 50

— ◆ —

*Step by step, we cooperate with God
in creating a life together.*

**STEP
BY
STEP**

When we united our hearts and our
minds, we were agreeing to create a
life together. Our communication with
and consideration for each other are
important steps in that building process.

How have we done so far? We may not know the
answer because we are focused on the activity that is
taking place around us or because we feel intimidated
just thinking about the future. Yet when we take one
day at a time, one step at a time, we bring our
responsibilities to each other, our family, and our careers
down to manageable proportions.

Acknowledging that God is our all-powerful, ever-
present partner, we remind ourselves that we are not in
this alone. We are always making progress when we
cooperate in a partnership with God. Step by step, we
are creating a life together.

"When you walk, your step will not be hampered;
and if you run, you will not stumble."
—Proverbs 4:12

Day 51

—◆—

Because we have been created by God,
we are priceless masterpieces.

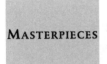

MASTERPIECES

Knowing that we are two priceless masterpieces in a world of masterpieces created by God, we value ourselves, each other, and all others.

The spirit of God emanates from within us as life and love. As children of God, we joyfully celebrate the life that God has given us.

We know that feeling good about ourselves and who we are is reflected in our life every day. We see ourselves as God's masterpieces, never doubting that we are precious to God and precious to each other.

Letting our faith in God bring us home to the truth of who we are, we enrich our relationship with sacredness. We give expression to God's greatness by being beloved friends and companions who bless each other, our family, and our friends.

"A friend loves at all times."
—Proverbs 17:17

Day 52

---◆---

*God guides us in speaking a wisdom of the heart
that promotes peace and understanding.*

**WORDS
OF LOVE**

There are times in our conversations when it is very, very difficult *not* to interrupt when the other is speaking. Yet an inner urging tells us to let the one who is talking finish. In that pause, we will learn more of what we need to know to form our thoughts and opinions.

This is especially true when, as we pause, we invite God to help us understand the situation and guide us in speaking a wisdom of the heart. Then our words are words of love and peace. We never want what we say to cause pain or misunderstanding, so we focus our words on the situation, not on the emotions that may prove later to be caused by a misunderstanding.

Words are powerful tools, and we want our conversations to be built from words that promote peace and understanding between us.

> **"Steadfast love and faithfulness will meet;
> righteousness and peace will kiss each other."**
> **—Psalms 85:10**

Day 53

—◆—

*God's love within us and between us is our expression
of true happiness.*

HAPPINESS The happiness we derive from
sharing life with each other does not
require that every day be filled with
fun and laughter. There is the
underlying current of joy we feel in being together in
the best of times and the most challenging of times.

Our Creator brought us together and guides us each
day in meeting divine appointments. Sharing a bond of
love for a lifetime, we reflect God's love within us and
God's love being shared by us as our true expressions of
happiness.

People see our smiles and hear our laughter as
indicators of the happiness we are feeling. Yet there is
within us, beneath the smiles and beyond the laughter,
the constant glow of God's love. That love warms our
hearts and brightens our time together. We are filled
with joy and happiness.

> "Let your adornment be the inner self with
> the lasting beauty of a gentle and quiet spirit."
> —1 Peter 3:4

Day 54

— ◆ —

Encouraging each other to be creative is a blessing
we both give and receive.

ENCOURAGING CREATIVITY We have faith in God and faith in God working through us in ways we know of and also in ways that we have yet to discover. Through our faith, we encourage each other to be creative in how we use our time and energy in our relationship, in our work, and toward our spiritual growth.

We feel such joy in watching each other succeed in learning a new skill or simply smoothing out a situation that might otherwise become awkward.

We feel blessed each time we acknowledge each other's talents and abilities. When we encourage each other with a compliment, a word of appreciation, or a smile, we feel good. And we know just the right things to say and do to encourage each other to keep on keeping on when we are working toward an important goal.

"I am sending him to you for this very purpose, to let you know how we are, and to encourage your hearts."
—Ephesians 6:22

Day 55

*Leaving the past behind, we are living
the wonderful realities that are ours today.*

**NO
REGRETS**

Today is a brand-new day—a day of new beginnings for us. This is a day that is filled with new opportunities to enhance ourselves and our relationship. From this moment on, let's live fully and freely. This means that we live in the newness of each moment without any regrets for mistakes of the past. From this moment on, we live each day as the gift from God that it truly is and look forward to a brighter future.

The beauty of leaving the past behind and living in the moment is that we are creating a better relationship. The understanding we share, the forgiveness we offer each other, and the guidance from God that we apply in keeping our relationship whole are the realities of today and every tomorrow.

**"Do not worry about anything, but in everything
by prayer and supplication with thanksgiving let
your requests be made known to God."
—Philippians 4:6**

Day 56

—◆—

We enrich our relationship by learning from each other and learning together about life.

LEARNING FROM EACH OTHER   We have learned so much about each other and from each other. Because we are willing to teach and be taught by example, our life together grows richer and fuller.

Giving the light touch, we find that humor does ease tension, offering some relief in what would otherwise be a stressful time. We are able to laugh together. Out of a deep, abiding respect, neither of us ridicules the other.

Working as a team, we help each other have a clearer understanding of our finances, responsibilities, and everyday life. Helping each other to bridge any gaps in our mutual understanding, we are making sure that no misunderstanding remains between us.

We are learning from each other and learning how blessed we are to have each other.

"Take my yoke upon you, and learn from me; for I am gentle and humble in heart, and you will find rest for your souls. For my yoke is easy, and my burden is light."
—Matthew 11:29–30

Day 57

—◆—

*Opening our hearts to the wisdom of God, we hear
the true message that is meant for us.*

**TRUE
MESSAGE**
An emotional reaction by one of us to what the other is saying may be from an impression of what was said, rather than the true message. What we need to do is listen so that we open our hearts and let God help us hear the true message.

We put aside our own personal feelings for a moment and really listen—not just to words but also to the true meaning behind those words. It helps us to listen with our eyes as well as our ears in order to understand.

The expression on the face of the one speaking may be saying, "I am having a difficult time saying what I want to say." A tone of voice may carry the unspoken message, "I am speaking with heartfelt sincerity." A loving look may also convey, "I'm listening and I really want to hear what you are saying."

As we continue to listen, we hear the true message that is meant for us.

"Listen to me; let me also declare my opinion."
—Job 32:10

Day 58

—◆—

*Our prayers link us heart and soul, no matter
how far apart we may be.*

**TIME
APART**

There may be nothing we enjoy
more than spending time together.
However we spend that time—
whether in quiet conversation or
working at home on our individual hobbies—we feel a
sense of completeness and contentment.

Yet there are times when we are apart, whether it is
because one of us leaves to travel across the country on
business or across town to take care of parents or other
family members. A short or extended time apart can
leave us feeling lonely for each other; yet it is also a time
to understand that distance can never come between us
and our love for each other.

In a time apart, we find relief from loneliness through
a telephone call or a letter. And our prayers are a
powerful link that unites us instantly—no matter how
far apart we may be.

**"The apostles gathered around Jesus, and told him all that
they had done and taught. He said to them, 'Come away
to a deserted place all by yourselves and rest a while.' "
—Mark 6:30–31**

Day 59

—◆—

Our Prayer

Dear God,

We know that You are always with us, yet we feel led to pray a special prayer for each other's safety and security in every undertaking today.

In Your presence, we are sheltered in a safe harbor of love and caring. We know that there is no person or no circumstance that can harm us because You are there.

No matter where we may go or what circumstances may arise, Your presence and power are there—surrounding and enfolding us in a haven of peace that only You can provide.

Thank You, Sweet Spirit, for guiding us and for enfolding this us in Your tender care.

"Do not fear, greatly beloved, you are safe.
Be strong and courageous!"
—Daniel 10:19

Day 60

—◆—

My Gift to You

I GIVE YOU THE GIFT OF HONORING YOUR HOPES AND DREAMS.

When we were first married, we had hopes and dreams that filled our hearts and heads with the endless possibilities that awaited us. Our dreams may change on occasion, because our priorities continue to change, but the hope will always be there. God is continually blessing us in more ways than we could ever have dreamed.

Today and every day, I honor your hopes and dreams by giving you my attention as you share them with me. Then I support you in achieving them.

With faith in God, I encourage you to dare to dream and to move forward to the possibilities that await you. No goal is unattainable for you as you give expression to the spirit of God within you.

> "Now faith is the assurance of things hoped for,
> the conviction of things not seen."
> —Hebrews 11:1

MAKING OUR COMMITMENT
A DAILY PRACTICE

BY JAYNE MEADOWS-ALLEN

Jumping out of a marriage is even more tragic than jumping into one, because I believe most marriages can be saved. When two people make honoring their commitment to each other a daily practice, they can make their marriage work.

My own parents made such a commitment. From all appearances, my mother and father were complete opposites. Dad was the son of Irish immigrants who came to America in the 1850s during the potato famine in Ireland. My mother's ancestors were wealthy Scottish aristocrats who had lived in America since the 1700s.

The two different worlds of my parents came together because of spirituality and romance. Mother was deeply religious, attending church in Mamaroneck, New York, with her parents every Sunday. Dad was the assistant minister that summer, and she said that when he stood in the pulpit to preach, "I had the strangest feeling in the pit of my stomach." She whispered to her father, "Let's invite Dr. Cotter to lunch." And they did.

Dad lunched at Mother's home almost every Sunday that summer, and they became engaged. Actually, it was Mother who talked Dad into going to China as a missionary.

He left for China a year ahead of Mother to learn the language and prepare for her arrival. She was chaperoned on her trip to the Orient by the vice president of the Standard Oil Company and his wife, close friends of my grandparents. The wedding took place in Yokahama, Japan, with eight Episcopalian Bishops in attendance. My parents honeymooned at a picturesque mountain resort above Tokyo.

The front page of the *New York Times* carried an article about Mother's departure, with this headline: "New York Socialite to Go to China to Work amongst Chinese Peasants!" Below the headline was a picture of my breathtakingly beautiful mother.

Mother and Dad spent the first 14 years of their marriage in China, giving their youth and health to China. They both contracted malaria many times. My two older brothers and I were born in Wu Chang. My sister, Audrey, was born in America when we came home on furlough.

Our mission, which Dad designed, is a replica of the Forbidden City and is, consequently, famous as the only Christian church in all China styled after traditional Chinese architecture. We had a clinic (a small hospital), and Chinese would come from great distances to be given free treatment. Dr. Wassell, the head of our clinic, became world famous years later. Cecil B. DeMille made a movie about his courageous evacuation of Bataan during the Second World War. Gary Cooper played Dr. Wassell in the movie, and I used to tease him about having delivered me, because the real-life Dr. Wassell did! And incidentally, gave me my name, Jayne.

Mother and Dad were a very attractive young couple. Chou En Lai, a communist leader, would often question our bishop, John Roots, "Why do you Christian foreigners come to our country? And why is this beautiful young couple interested in helping Chinese poor?" He was suspicious of Americans but realized that, although we were on totally different paths, we were trying to ease the suffering of the downtrodden peasants. I was 6 years old when we fled in the middle of the night. We were ordered to leave China by our American government. This was just before the Japanese invasion of China.

Thousands of foreigners were fleeing from China, and we ended up living for months in two rooms in a warehouse in Shanghai. Mother cooked all our meals over a grate fire, in tin food cans. When we finally made it to America, we settled in Providence, Rhode Island, and Dad became the first dean of St. John's Cathedral of Rhode Island.

My parents were magnificent role models. They taught me by example that two people can face and overcome great obstacles when they keep a daily commitment to each other.

These two shining examples were deeply spiritual people who loved each other and were dedicated to making their marriage work. Although my husband, Steve, and I had come from quite different backgrounds, there was always a foundation of faith and commitment that supported us through the joys and challenges of a marriage of 47 years.

We met quite accidentally. I had been under contract to MGM making movies in Hollywood but wanted to return to the New York stage. I was called for an audition of a new television show, "I've Got a Secret." Practically every actor and actress in New York was also auditioning. Fortunately, I learned to be an expert at playing games during my early years in China. This was how the other children and I entertained ourselves. So I not only got the job, I was signed on the spot to a 7-year contract!

Audrey had asked me to join her and some mutual friends at a restaurant after the audition. I was sitting at the table chattering away when I noticed a tall, dark, and handsome man enter the room. It was Steve Allen, whom I had seen on television many times. I took one look and made a mental note: "If that man's not married, he's going to be, and to me, someday!"

Steve joined our table, sitting in the only empty seat, which happened to be next to mine. He never spoke to me directly during the whole evening, but I caught him sneaking peeks at me when he thought I wasn't looking. He knew Audrey and the others, and as we were leaving, he walked over to Audrey and said, "Let's go to Sardi's for dessert, and bring your sister along." That's when I realized that this tall, dark, and handsome man was also painfully shy.

Steve and I got to really know each other slowly that summer, and I think this was crucial to our having a long-lasting relationship. There is a deep sense of commitment and caring when two people can be what we in show business call a "backup" for each other. We made a daily commitment to understanding each other in every way possible. When difficult times came in our marriage—as they do in practically all marriages—we were able to support each other emotionally. There are times when everyone needs the help of family and true friends. Fortunately we had them.

Times have changed, the world has changed between the time my mother and father and Steve and I were married. Yet I believe the commitment in both marriages made them work—whether in an isolated mission in China or in the hectic arena of show business.

Day 61

—◆—

*Our life together is an unfolding story of love
and prayer support.*

UNFOLDING STORY Picturing our life together as an unfolding story of two people who love and respect each other gives us greater insight into what we have accomplished together. God has a plan, and our meeting was no coincidence.

All that we have accomplished together happened as we followed a divine plan, not our own personal agendas. The beauty of it all is that our story is still unfolding. There is more in this divine plan than either one of us can imagine. Following where our Creator leads us, we move forward and discover the wonder that awaits us.

Our experiences are varied, but the joy of being together is such a blessing. Most important, our love and prayer support is a theme that is woven throughout our story.

"And now faith, hope, and love abide, these three;
and the greatest of these is love."
—1 Corinthians 13:13

Day 62

—◆—

Working as a team, we help each other and work together in maintaining our home.

MAINTAINING OUR HOME The upkeep of our home requires an investment of our time and skills, and our best investment is made while working together as a team.

Having a well-thought-out plan as to how we will work as a team helps us to get our jobs done and to be considerate of each other. Remembering that the head of our team is God, we know to be open to divine guidance in organizing and maintaining our home.

Sometimes we just need to cooperate in making decisions about the simplest housekeeping and repair jobs. If one of us enjoys a certain task more than the other one does, the decision is fairly easy. Taking turns may be the answer for doing the projects that neither one of us likes to do.

Whatever our decisions are, we carry them out as a team, helping each other and working together.

> **"Pray for us as well that God will open to us a door for the word."**
> **—Colossians 4:3**

Day 63

———◆———

In daily communion with God, we are guided on safe and secure pathways.

SAFE AND SECURE

When we listen for the voice of wisdom, we *feel* more than *hear* the reassurance we need. Although we may be most aware of God when we are quiet and focused, we know that God is always aware of us and communicating with us.

This sacred communication guides us on safe pathways throughout our life. Our decisions, actions, and responses are founded on our faith in God and God's ever-present guidance.

No detail we could ever pray about is too insignificant for God's attention. No challenge we could ever encounter is too great for God's power working in and for us to overcome.

We listen for divine guidance, for through our day-to-day, moment-to-moment communion with God, we are safe and secure.

"Jesus answered . . . 'My sheep hear my voice.
I know them, and they follow me.
I give them eternal life.'"
—John 10:25, 27–28

Day 64

—◆—

Forgiveness opens our way to a richer, healthier,
and more satisfying life.

FORGIVENESS
HEALS

Within our hearts, we know the healing power of forgiveness. However, we may be so focused on our feelings of hurt and disappointment that we don't even consider being forgiving.

What relief we feel when we allow forgiveness to bring greater peace and love into our life. So we pray each day for the wisdom to be more understanding and for the ability to forgive ourselves and each other.

As we forgive, we are giving from the love of God within us. We realize the blessings of forgiveness as our relationship improves. Forgiveness opens the way for an exchange of clear communication and inspires us to get along.

We sense a healing within us and within our relationship. Forgiveness enables us to live a richer, healthier, and more satisfying life.

"Pray for one another, so that you may be healed."
—James 5:16

Day 65

God loves us unconditionally.

GRACE Just as we are today, God loves us. There has never been, nor will there ever be a time when God does not love us unconditionally.

The unconditional love of God is grace—something we have never earned nor will we ever have to earn. Grace blesses our relationship, assuring us that we are worthy of God's love and that we are worthy of giving and receiving love.

God loves us just as we are. We need do nothing to keep God's love; however, knowing that we are loved the way we are inspires us to always try to do better.

Each time we honor each other by loving each other just as we are—without any attempt by either of us to change the other—we are not placing any conditions on our love.

Loving each other as we are, we will continue to love each other always.

> "By the grace of God I am what I am, and his grace toward me has not been in vain."
> —1 Corinthians 15:10

Day 66

—◆—

*United in a sacred bond, we love
and understand each other.*

**SACRED
BOND**

We are united by a sacred bond that links us heart to heart and soul to soul. Because we call on love and wisdom to be involved in every decision we make about being a couple and about being individuals, we make and act on decisions that are important to our relationship and our individuality.

We are motivated by what the spirit of God inspires us to do, not by what we feel we are obligated to do. Because we are spiritually motivated, we think, speak, and act on what enriches us and our life together.

Because we are united in a sacred bond, nothing can cause our relationship to come apart. We live from a center of love that would not and could not let us disregard our commitment to each other and to our family. Our sacred bond lights up our life with understanding and purpose.

**"There is one body and one Spirit, just as you were called
to the one hope of your calling, one Lord, one faith,
one baptism, one God and Father of all, who is above all
and through all and in all."—Ephesians 4:4–6**

Day 67

—◆—

God is with us.

MOVING

Moving the contents of our entire household to a new location, no matter what the distance, can be a stressful experience. Cooperating as we work, we will help each other avoid becoming stressed. We recognize potential problems and then eliminate them. Prayer is a great eliminator of stress. So we pray before we sign papers to sell or buy a house or begin to pack for a move.

God is the assurance that we seek and the strength that we need to complete the move. Fortified by our faith, we know that our move and everything connected with it will progress smoothly and efficiently. God will see us through.

The presence of God goes before us, preparing our way. God will be with us in our new house as a presence of love and peace that makes it our home.

> "The uneven ground shall become level,
> and the rough places a plain."
> —Isaiah 40:4

Day 68

—◆—

*Our positive outlook on life inspires us
to recognize and accept blessings.*

**GREAT
OVERCOMING** There is a saying that when life
hands you a lemon, make lemonade.
This reminds us of the positive ways
we have handled some seemingly
negative situations. Together we have been able to
make something good out of those times life presented
us with challenges.

Being positive is a practical way of not letting
disappointment and fear keep us from working through
a challenge together. We believe that God brought us
together so that we could be helpmates in overcoming
challenges and in perceiving the blessings that are
always there for us. Being together side by side, we
know that our love gives us an extra boost of courage.
Looking back, we understand that we have a proven
history of what we have accomplished together.
Looking forward, we have faith in all that we *can*
accomplish together.

**"Do not fear, only believe."
—Mark 5:36**

Day 69

◆

We let go and let God.

LET GO, LET GOD
We do all we know to do to resolve any challenge we may face. There are, however, some situations that are beyond the realm of our understanding. So we release them into God's loving care.

If there is a healing need, we visualize ourselves as God created us to be—whole and well. We hold an image of ourselves full of life and vitality, knowing that the presence of God is powerfully at work, healing and restoring us.

Concerning a financial or emotional challenge, we see ourselves free of worry and stress. We give the challenge to God for divine results. In letting go and letting God, we are not giving up; we are giving our full attention to God and the divine solution that will be revealed to us.

All this we do as we let go and let God.

"And now, O Lord, as for the word that you have spoken concerning your servant and concerning his house, let it be established forever, and do as you have promised."
—1 Chronicles 17:23

Day 70

—◆—

*We are thankful that we live in
a world of God's wonder.*

**WE ARE
GRATEFUL!** We may have started out together
with few possessions, but we have
been blessed by the riches of God's
creativity. Giving thanks for what we
have is one of the best ways to lift our spirits and
improve our outlook on life. So every day we express
our gratitude for the opportunity to live in a world of
God's wonder.

We are grateful for the sun and the moon and the
stars and for this magnificent planet on which we live.
The light of the sun and the beauty of the moon and
stars remind us that God's love and power are without
limit.

We are grateful for the food we eat, for the clothes we
wear, and for a home that provides shelter and warmth.
And we are especially thankful for each other and for
family and friends who share our life and our joy.

"Be glad and rejoice forever in what I am creating;
for I am about to create Jerusalem as a joy,
and its people as a delight."
—Isaiah 65:18

Day 71

—◆—

*Lowering our defenses helps us
live together in harmony.*

**LOWERING
DEFENSES** Sometimes it only takes a word or a
look from one of us to cause the other
to shift into a defensive attitude.
Lowering our defenses may take some
time and effort, yet it makes our life so much smoother.

Being involved in a relationship isn't easy, and we
certainly do not expect that we will *never* disagree with
each other. What we do expect and rely on is that, if
we disagree, we do it in a calm and accepting manner.

So we make a conscious effort to lower our defenses
and to allow the love of God to flow through us and
out from us. Because our lives are deeply rooted in
faith, we know that no outer circumstance has the
power to disturb our inner peace.

Through this one simple act of release, we allow
God's love to shine forth from us so that we live
together in harmony.

> "Bless the Lord, O my soul, and do not forget
> all his benefits . . . who crowns you
> with steadfast love and mercy."
> —Psalms 103:2–4

Day 72

———◆———

*Thank God, our lives are filled
with extraordinary moments.*

**EXTRA-
ORDINARY
MOMENTS**

If we were to keep a memory book of all the important moments in our life, we would be certain to write down each extraordinary moment that we have shared.

The day that we met, the time that we pledged our love and faith to each other before God, and the date that we came together as a family—all are extraordinary moments that we will treasure forever.

Each day is a day that we can celebrate the joy and wonder of being together. Every moment may not necessarily be extraordinary, but we can give thanks for even the ordinary events, such as quiet, peaceful times of rest and relaxation.

Every day we are filling a blank page of the memory book of our life together, and we still have many adventures and momentous occasions yet to experience and to celebrate.

> **"Come, let us walk in the light of the Lord!"**
> **—Isaiah 2:5**

Day 73

*Building our life together, we follow a blueprint
of our commitment to each other and to God.*

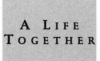

**A LIFE
TOGETHER**

A well-constructed house stands
as a testament that a sound blueprint
was followed, quality material was
used, and caring people were involved
in building it.

Our life together stands as a testament also that we
are following a blueprint for a fulfilling life, giving our
best in living it and caring about each other as we do.
We are building on the solid foundation of our faith in
God. No matter what situations may arise, we have
faith that sustains us.

Because inner peace is so vitally important to our well-
being, we ask God, "How do we handle this?" whenever
a challenge presents itself. The answer always comes:
"You will never need to handle this or anything else on
your own. I am with you to guide and protect you."

**"Lead a life worthy of the calling to which you have been
called, with all humility and gentleness, with patience,
bearing with one another in love, making every effort
to maintain the unity of the Spirit in the bond of peace."
—Ephesians 4:1–3**

Day 74

——◆——

Our Prayer

Dear God,

We are grateful for Your order, which is actively at work in our life and in the lives of our loved ones. We feel the powerful, wonderful effects of Your order in resolving the challenges of unplanned or unexpected occurrences.

Thank You, God, for showing us that there is always a solution to every problem, for Your presence is moving through every circumstance and situation as order that brings about a divine answer. Thank You for reminding us that we don't have to have the answer; we just need to be willing to listen to and follow Your guidance.

Knowing that You are always with us and our family, we look for and discover the order that underlies every action and event. We trust in You in every moment and in every circumstance.

"The one who comes from above is above all; the one who is of the earth belongs to the earth and speaks about earthly things. The one who comes from heaven is above all."
—John 3:31

Day 75

—◆—

My Gift to You

I GIVE YOU THE GIFT OF MY PATIENCE.

Being caught in bumper-to-bumper traffic and late for an appointment or work, we probably won't feel peace-filled or serene. At such a stressful time, I give you the comforting gift of my patience. I choose to relax and turn this time of waiting into a quiet time of conversation with you.

We can think of this pause in our schedule as an opportunity to take a prayer break together—a few moments of knowing that we are being held in the loving embrace of God's tender care.

Wherever we are, God is there also. Even though God already knows what is on our minds and in hearts, we are blessed in finding an extra moment to have time together and time with God. I am grateful for this time and for the opportunity to give you the gift of my patience.

"The fruit of the Spirit is love, joy, peace, patience, kindness, generosity, faithfulness, gentleness, and self-control."
—Galatians 5:22

Day 76

♦

We are reflections of the love of God.

DAYS OF RAINBOWS Seeing a rainbow arch across the sky after a rain shower, we are reminded of the majesty of God's world. This breathtaking display fills us with renewed hope, and we come away from the experience with the feeling that all things are possible.

Yet whether or not a rainbow makes an appearance, each day is one filled with promise for us. We know that in God's presence, there is always hope. God is with us and love is with us, and in the presence of God and God's love, we remain calm and secure.

A rainbow is created by reflected light, and we, too, reflect the light of God. We bring all of the joy and peace we feel to our relationship and do our utmost to ensure that every day is a day of rainbows. We allow the love of God to be a part of every conversation that we have and every moment that we share together.

> "This is the day that the Lord has made;
> let us rejoice and be glad in it."
> —Psalms 118:24

Day 77

—◆—

*In the solitude of prayer, we invite divine love
to soothe our souls.*

**TEARING
DOWN
WALLS**

A first reaction by one of us to the other's solution to a dilemma may be to put up a wall of resistance—refusing to talk any longer about the situation and how we can solve it. Once a wall is in place, it hinders meaningful communication.

At such a time, we may need to be alone in our own space for a while so that we can quiet our thoughts and pray about the situation. It is in the solitude of prayer that we let the wall of resistance come down and invite divine love to soothe our souls and vanquish any negative thoughts.

With God's love showing us the way, we are once again open and receptive to what each other has to suggest. The stumbling blocks are gone, and we can move forward in a positive and loving way in reaching a solution on which we can both agree.

> "You hold my right hand.
> You guide me with your counsel."
> —Psalms 73:23–24

Day 78

— ◆ —

Surrendering to God, we work in partnership with the One Power in the universe.

SURRENDER The word *surrender* may bring to mind the thought of giving up something we are reluctant to give up. However, when we surrender ourselves completely and wholly to God, we discover that we are not giving up anything at all. Rather we are working in partnership with God.

In surrendering to God, we are giving over to our Creator those things with which we may have been struggling. As we release concerns to God, we feel such a blessed relief, for we know we will never have to go through anything without the help of God.

God is our divine partner, who is guiding us, loving us, and nurturing us. Surrendering to God, we acknowledge that the One Power in all the universe is in charge. God is the presence and power to which we surrender all.

> "That which is, already has been;
> that which is to be, already is."
> —Ecclesiastes 3:15

Day 79

—◆—

*God gives us the insight and understanding
we need to follow a divine plan.*

BLESSINGS IN DISGUISE We understand that there are people and events that affect us in profound ways and move us forward in our relationship.

Our family and friends help us create an environment of love in which we live and relate to one another. When we are together, we serve as examples of how love looks in expression.

Even though we may not have been aware of it at the time, we now can look at past events and realize that some of the challenges we faced were actually blessings in disguise. They were opportunities for us to gain a better understanding of God and also a better understanding of each other.

God has plans for us, and we trust God to give us the insight and understanding we need to keep on keeping on.

> "For the Lord gives wisdom; from his mouth
> come knowledge and understanding."
> —Proverbs 2:6

Day 80

—◆—

*As we share laughter, we are also sharing
a time of expressing the joy of our souls.*

LAUGHING TOGETHER Like a tonic, laughter can invigorate us. As we laugh, we release any tension that we may have been feeling and replace it with joy. As we laugh together, our hearts fairly sing with the joy we share.

Laughter is contagious—when one of us hears the other laughing, we feel our hearts lighten and our spirits soar, until we both are laughing together. And when something strikes us as funny and we feel laughter building up inside us, we immediately want to share the experience with each other.

As laughter surges forth from us, we are rejuvenated and refreshed. The sound of each other's laughter lifts our spirits, and we experience a heightened awareness of God. This happens because the spirit of God is a well-spring of joy that flows forth through our laughter.

> "Worship the Lord with gladness;
> come into his presence with singing."
> —Psalms 100:2

Day 81

—◆—

Our willingness to cooperate with God and with each other is reflected in our life.

WHAT GOD CAN DO

When our life is going smoothly, we may find it easy to get along with each other. Living and working in harmony doesn't seem much of a challenge. Yet the loss of a job means one less paycheck and can test our ability to cooperate with each other and to even cope with what is happening.

Coming through a lifestyle change or a crisis as a loving, devoted couple shows what God can do through us when we are willing to follow divine guidance.

Our willingness to cooperate with God and with each other is reflected in our everyday life and unites us during a crisis. We each have contributed to keeping our relationship whole. United in faith, love, and purpose, we have withstood challenges. Strengthened by our commitment to remain united, we are continuing on.

"But those who wait for the Lord shall renew their strength, they shall mount up with wings like eagles, they shall run and not be weary, they shall walk and not faint."—Isaiah 40:31

Day 82

—◆—

*Our thoughts reach out to each other
on the wings of our prayers.*

**UNITED
IN
THOUGHT** Thought after thought of each other
reminds us of how much we mean to
each other. Our thoughts are prayers,
for they are declarations of health,
safety, and peace.

We know when we are thinking of each other, for
our prayers help us throughout the day. So as we hold
thoughts of peace, we are a tremendous support for
each other.

Knowing that we are thinking of each other and
devoting time to helping each other, we are doubly
blessed. Our thoughts are messages of love and support
that are carried on the wings of prayer. In fact, there are
times when we experience a peaceful sensation and
know we have just been touched by a loving thought.
What a wonderful feeling that is!

> **"You ride on the wings of the wind, you make
> the winds your messengers."**
> **—Psalms 104:3–4**

Day 83

---◆---

Giving our faith and attention to God,
we help create a special day.

SPECIAL DAY

Every moment that we are together is one to be cherished, and what we give to this day more than what this day gives to us makes it a special day.

So we give our faith to God through our positive attitude and conversations. The faith we have expressed returns to us as greater peace of mind, which can only improve our relationship.

We give our attention to God and not to the challenges. Our focus on the sacred Presence in every situation reveals the beauty and majesty in people and situations that may have seemed ordinary and routine.

When we give our faith and attention to God, the blessings of every day are revealed. We rejoice together as we give from the life, love, and understanding of God's presence within us to this day.

> **"Glory in his holy name; let the hearts**
> **of those who seek the Lord rejoice."**
> **—Psalms 105:3**

DAILY WORD FOR COUPLES

Day 84

*We make it through the seasons of our life
strengthened by our love and faith.*

**OUR
SEASONS**

The beginning of a new season may
be marked by subtle or dramatic
changes in the weather and the
environment. We feel especially close
to each other during those times that together we watch
silent snow falling on our lawn or listen to rain tapping
on our windows.

We feel so close as we go through the seasons of our
life also. We are changing and the world is changing, yet
we are going through it all together. The spirit of God
within us is expressing wisdom, life, and creativity
through us. We understand that life is so much easier
for us because we are sharing both the challenges and
the joys.

Some seasons of life may seem more difficult than
others, but we have not despaired nor will we despair.
Our love for each other and our faith in God keep us
strengthened and keep us together.

> **"They are like trees planted by streams of water,
> which yield their fruit in its season."**
> **—Psalms 1:3**

DAILY WORD FOR COUPLES

Day 85

---◆---

The more we appreciate each other,
the more we discover to appreciate.

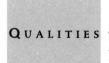

QUALITIES We compile all kinds of lists; grocery, birthday, and appointment lists are just a few. Yet there are two lists that are as important as all the rest: our lists of each other's qualities.

Once in a while, we may make a mental or written list of things we each appreciate about the other. It's as if God is saying, "The more you discover to appreciate in each other, the more you find to appreciate!"

There is so much about each other to value. We appreciate that we share the responsibility of making our marriage work and that we are generous in all that we do in helping with our family. We appreciate that we are companions who can bounce ideas off each other and know that we will be given constructive feedback. We thank God for reminding us to express our appreciation—often.

"The beginning of wisdom is this: Get wisdom, and whatever else you get, get insight. Prize her highly, and she will exalt you; she will honor you if you embrace her." —Proverbs 4:7–8

Day 86

$\longrightarrow \blacklozenge \longrightarrow$

In silent prayer, we are open to ways
of communicating with understanding.

IN SILENCE   Sometimes deciding whether to talk or not talk to each other when we are having a problem communicating can be a real dilemma. Talking while we are emotional, we might say things that we don't mean and that we will later regret. Yet by not talking, we may each feel as though the other is shutting us out.

Still we can be silent and help ourselves to gain composure and understanding. Praying in silence is a powerful way to open us to being considerate of each other and to open meaningful communication.

Spending time in the same room in silent prayer, we convey our intention to bring a sacredness to our time together. We may start in silence with a simple request: "God help us to help each other." Being totally in the presence of God for a few moments, we are relieved of anger and ready to be understanding and to be understood.

> **"For God alone my soul waits in silence;**
> **from him comes my salvation."**
> **—Psalms 62:1**

Day 87

◆

God is guiding us with a divine plan
for this day and every day.

GUIDANCE When we feel sure about a decision we have made, we will not hesitate to move forward with it. When even a bit of doubt invades our thoughts, however, a decision may soon cause us to feel anxious.

Yet how do we know that our decisions are sound and wise? We pray every day so that we are open to divine wisdom every day, not just when we are facing a challenge. Prayer refreshes our minds, eases tension in our bodies, and invites God to be part of our every decision.

Prayer offers us relief from emotional discomfort and physical pain. In our sacred times of communion with God, we are guided to ideas that bless us as we use them in setting goals and making everyday plans. The presence of God leads us, and we follow.

"You are indeed my rock and my fortress;
for your name's sake lead me and guide me."
—Psalms 31:3

DAILY WORD FOR COUPLES

Day 88

—◆—

As friends, we live together in an atmosphere
of love and acceptance.

FRIENDS Our friendship means that we are good to each other and good for each other. As friends, we have created an atmosphere in which we accept and love each other as we are. Yet within such an atmosphere, we are encouraged to become even more as individuals and for each other.

We nourish our relationship, so that, as time goes by, we become even closer and more trusting. We have learned so much about each other, and our relationship is stronger because we have given and received love and forgiveness, appreciation, and compassion.

We know the unique qualities that attracted us to each other in the beginning, but it is friendship that draws us even closer. We are friends and companions who walk beside each other, blessing each other's journey through life.

"This is my commandment, that you love one another
as I have loved you. No one has greater love than this,
to lay down one's life for one's friends."
—John 15:12–13

Day 89

$\blacklozenge$

Our Prayer

Dear God,

You bless our home with love so that all who enter through these doors immediately feel the assurance of Your presence and Your peace.

More than mere wood, glass, or brick, our home is a place where our loved ones can come and share in a time of togetherness and caring. It is here that we spend our hours of rest and relaxation, and we want all who come here to feel the love we have for each other and the love we feel for You.

God, You bless the food that we eat—so that it nourishes and sustains our bodies and keeps us healthy and fit.

God, You bless our beloved pets who share their lives and their love with us. May they long be a source of joy and happiness in our lives.

God, thank You for our home and for the joy and laughter that echo within its walls.

**"Even the sparrow finds a home . . .
at your altars, O Lord of hosts."
—Psalms 84:3**

Day 90

◆

My Gift to You

**I GIVE YOU THE GIFT
OF FORGIVENESS.**

So much of what forgiveness is about is letting go of the emotions that everyday differences stir up. Often the feeling of anger is remembered but the details of what caused it are forgotten.

Whether it is by my words or my actions that I am conveying forgiveness, I am pledging that I am not holding on to any thought of resentment or anger about anything you have done or have not done. I am doing something that blesses me as much as I hope it blesses you: By being forgiving, I am letting God express love and understanding through me.

I am putting aside my own tendency to be judgmental so that I am not judging you based on my expectations of what you should do and how you should act. As much as I love you, I can never know exactly what you are facing. By being nonjudgmental, I am saying that I love you and I support you in being all that God is leading you to be.

"Be at peace among yourselves."
—1 Thessalonians 5:13

DAILY WORD FOR COUPLES

Preparing for Life Prepares Us for Marriage

By Steve Allen

I didn't have the good fortune of being born into a family like that of my wife, Jayne—through nobody's fault. Nobody sets out to be a bad wife or husband or mother or father, but nevertheless, some people fall into these categories.

Unfortunately, my father died when I was 1½ years old, so he had a negligible effect on me. By all reports, which is all I know of him, he was very nice and sweet.

My mother, on the other hand, was more to the opposite end of that particular scale. She had many charms, one of which was her wonderful Irish sense of humor. She was an entertainer, and comedian Milton Berle, who worked with her as a teenager, described her as the funniest woman in Vaudeville. As funny as she was on stage, she was, when in a good mood, even funnier at home.

Her comedic talent certainly was a plus for me. Whether it is the result of genetic factors or just some social conditioning, my own humor was influenced by my mother's.

In the role of mother, however, she left a great deal to be desired. Part of it was not her fault because her profession did not allow her to be a full-time mother. She would spend 4 to 5 days in Des Moines, then another 4 to 5 in Chicago. She worked in 75 to 80 cities in a year. Although this kind of work had its attractions, it was a poor context within which to try to raise a child.

First of all, it would have been tough for her alone to get from Terre Haute to Indianapolis in the best of circumstances. It would have been worse having a crying toddler along while she was sitting at a depot all night waiting for the 4:00 A.M. train to come through. Then a whole new order of difficulties would have clicked into place when I became 5. According to law, I had to go to school. This meant that my mother was on the road in Vaudeville getting standing ovations in Chicago, but not seeing me for months at a time.

I was left behind with my mother's friends and our relatives until I was around 9. Then I was sent to a Catholic boarding school, where there was a strong emphasis on spirituality and morality. The nuns helped me, and years later, I returned the favor by teaching religion classes and kept in touch with the nuns who befriended me.

During my teenage years, I lived with my mother. I believe there is powerful instruction in both good and

DAILY WORD FOR COUPLES

bad examples. I didn't drink or smoke. The reason is very clear: I saw so much of it in the home, for my mother drank and smoked heavily.

There was some minor social disgrace to both habits at the time I was a teen. My poor mother was so addicted to tobacco that she smoked on the street, and my friends saw it. She was the only mother within our social circle who smoked.

I have had friends, clergy, psychiatrists, all trying to figure out how I could have come from that background and still not have become an alcoholic or worse. Jayne always said it was because God gave me talent—a strange complex of abilities for the composition of music, playing the piano, and writing poetry, short stories, and plays. Though I have written over 8,000 songs, I never learned to read music.

So perhaps it's all of those things—the comedy, the acting, the writing—that covered a multitude of sins, or, at least, kept me out of trouble. I recognize the abilities, but don't feel that I deserve any credit for my gifts. There are people in life who deserve tremendous credit and never get it except through their close friends and family.

There was a story that was known to teenagers of my generation that can bring tears to your eyes just thinking of it. It concerns a man who, in the 1930s, was a famous athlete. Glenn Cunningham held the world's record in the 1-mile track event. The road to this great achievement was not an easy one. When he was a child, he was caught in a fire. He was rescued at the last possible minute but suffered severe burns on his feet and legs. The doctors told his parents that Glenn might never walk again. They added that, if he were able to walk, it probably would be with the aid of braces and crutches.

Well, that was chapter 1 of his life. In chapter 37, Glenn Cunningham crossed the finish line in the Olympics as the fastest miler on Earth. He started so far behind the starting line and still achieved greatness.

My point in telling his story is that I don't think I deserve any gold medals for my talents. But perhaps Jayne is right in saying that talent saved me. I was busy doing things that other young people weren't doing. I may not have consciously known what I wanted to do with my life, but I knew what I did not want to do with it.

Like life, a marriage can be thrown away for various reasons. It ought to be impressed on young people, literally from first-grade level, that their eventual fate may be to get married and that it is a very difficult process. Starting from the first time we meet the person who in 20 days or 12 years will become our mates, we need to know that our relationships are not going to be like those portrayed in the movies or TV shows, where a couple has a few dates and lives happily ever after.

That's not how life is. And even on the lovely day we are married and drive off into the sunset together, sud-

DAILY WORD FOR COUPLES

denly on the way home, our car can get smashed. Or later on, a child can be born with a disability. The possibilities for tragedy are not only occasionally encountered, they are all around us every day. If they don't affect us, they affect our brothers-in-law or our neighbors. So we cannot escape life. A very common title for sermons is "Why do bad things happen to good people?"

This subject is addressed in the Bible in the book of Job. It is shocking to some people to hear that the question has really never been answered. It's good that we raise the question and wrestle with it, so that hopefully we can accept it as a part of life. Bad things do indeed happen to good people too.

I have long advocated that preparation for marriage and all the stages that lead to it should be incorporated into our formal educational system. To an extent, churches do this, but much more is needed. Although I have learned to eliminate certain habits from my life because I had a bad example before me, I believe even more strongly that good examples and training can bring out a talent, so to speak, for being a good wife or husband, for being a good mother, father, or citizen.

Life is full of choices, and even when we don't have the good examples and early training to help us, we have the innate ability to make choices that support ourselves and our loved ones.

Day 91
— ◆ —

We are refreshed in a time of giving thanks
for our blessings from God.

SHOWERS
OF
BLESSINGS
When we become caught up in our day-to-day responsibilities and routines, we may not be aware of how blessed we are.

All this changes when we take a break from thinking about and working on a special project or simply thinking about and working on everyday life. We then begin to consider our blessings. It's amazing, for we soon discover that we have so many blessings for which to be thankful.

How refreshed we are in taking time out each day to look for and give thanks for our blessings. Like the first few raindrops before a downpour, the first few blessings come to mind slowly—one by one—and then a virtual shower of blessings takes place.

> "Come, you that are blessed by my Father,
> inherit the kingdom prepared for you
> from the foundation of the world."
> —Matthew 25:34

Day 92

◆

*We are honest with each other in kind
and loving ways.*

HONESTY

We have heard this expression many times: my word is my bond. We want to know that our word is our bond, so we promise to be open and honest with each other.

We feel so at ease with each other because we have built a trust in each other. When we ask for an opinion, we know that is exactly what we want to hear. Yet, just because we have a certain opinion about a matter doesn't mean that we expect our views on it to be the same.

We can be honest because our love is strong enough to handle differences. Whatever we say is said in a kind and loving way.

We love each other, and because we do, we are open and honest with each other.

> "Lead me in your truth, and teach me,
> for you are the God of my salvation."
> —Psalms 25:5

Day 93

—◆—

*Our spiritual roots keep us firmly grounded
in our faith in God.*

SPIRITUAL ROOTS
Looking at a mighty oak tree, we can only imagine the vast expanse of roots that lay hidden below ground. Those roots go very deep within the ground, sustaining and supporting the part of the tree that we are able to see and touch.

Our lives are founded in the presence of God, so we share spiritual roots that support and strengthen us. Despite what is happening, we remain firmly grounded in our faith in God. No person or situation will ever uproot us spiritually.

The spirit of God is expressing life and love through us—unseen and yet powerful enough to sustain us at every moment. God provides us with the very breath that we breathe and all the wisdom we need to live life fully.

> "They shall flourish as a garden;
> they shall blossom like the vine."
> —Hosea 14:7

Day 94

—◆—

We create an atmosphere of love in our home
that blesses our family.

WORKING PARENTS There are times when it seems as if our work commitments outside our home do not give us enough time to fulfill our responsibilities to each other and the rest of our family. Yet in a cooperation of love and support, we work together to give each other and our family care and attention.

Our family is important to us, and we express our love in words and with actions that let everyone know how much we care about and appreciate one another.

We make the time we have together count by listening to what our loved ones have to say, encouraging them to follow their dreams and supporting them in achieving their goals.

Being working parents is not easy, yet we know that with God's support and our combined efforts, we create an atmosphere of love in our home that blesses us all.

> **"For where your treasure is, there**
> **your heart will be also."**
> **—Matthew 6:21**

Day 95

—◆—

In a time of silent prayer,
we nourish our souls.

NOURISHING OUR SOULS
We know that in order to nourish ourselves physically, we need to eat nutritious meals, but how do we nourish ourselves spiritually? Reserving time each day for prayer and meditation, we satisfy the hunger of our souls for divine inspiration.

Just as we share a family meal together, we can also share a family prayer time together. Settling into comfortable chairs, we draw energy from each other's comforting presence. Closing our eyes, we say a silent prayer and recognize God as a loving presence in our family relationships.

Prayer is a way of releasing concerns and tension that would otherwise cause us problems. Prayer is also a way of acknowledging that God is in charge of our lives. As we pray, a feeling of peace settles over us. Our souls are nourished in our time of prayer.

> "Beloved, I pray that all may go well
> with you and that you may be in good health,
> just as it is well with your soul."
> —3 John 1:2

Day 96

—◆—

*The light of God is understanding
that guides us in making decisions.*

**OUR
GUIDING
LIGHT**
On a foggy day or at night, the beacon from a lighthouse cuts through the fog or darkness to alert ships about nearby rocks and shoreline.

The guiding light we receive from God is not limited to just our vision. God's light is more powerful and far reaching. When we clear our minds of intrusive thoughts and close our eyes and ears to any disruptions, we will sense that God's guiding light is within our souls.

God will guide us in making decisions. Whether they seem momentous or trivial, all our decisions are important. The wisdom of God will always reveal the right answers to us. In all that we do, we have the benefit of divine understanding that enables us to see through any cloud of confusion to the blessed reality that is there for us.

> "Send out your light and your truth;
> let them lead me; let them bring me
> to your holy hill and to your dwelling."
> —Psalms 43:3

Day 97

— ◆ —

*Thank God for our journeys
of love and togetherness.*

**OUR
JOURNEYS**

Taking a moment for a break from the day, let's consider the amazing journeys we have made so far in our lives.

Growing up, we daydreamed about what we wanted to do with our lives. Chances are, we have not fulfilled some of those dreams, but we have discovered the benefits of not trying to limit our experiences by asking God for specific things to happen. We are open to God's will and give thanks every day that God's plan is so much greater than anything we ever could have envisioned for ourselves.

Our being together is a perfect example of the unfoldment of God's love and wisdom. So we say "thank you" to God and to each other. We do not have to travel alone, for we are together, and God accompanies us both.

> **"If we live by the Spirit, let us also
> be guided by the Spirit."
> —Galatians 5:25**

Day 98

◆

However far apart we may be,
we are united in spirit.

UNITED IN SPIRIT

Even though we enjoy spending time together, there may be times when we each feel the need to be alone with our thoughts. During those times, we do not feel as though we love each other any less, because nothing could be further from the truth. Even though we are not together physically, we do share a unity of spirit—a sense of togetherness that comes from being so attuned to each other.

Whatever physical distance may separate us, God is a sacred and powerful presence that unites us in spirit and love. God's love for both of us is the assurance that God's presence is always with us and that the peace we seek is always available to us.

God's presence keeps us emotionally and spiritually close even though we may be miles apart, for we share a unity of spirit.

"But you are not in the flesh; you are in the Spirit, since the Spirit of God dwells in you."
—Romans 8:9

Day 99

—◆—

*Thank You, God, for the diversity
within our family.*

DIVERSITY We are unique and different in our own ways. We welcome the expression of individuality in our relationship and we encourage diversity to flourish within our family.

Our children, parents, siblings, or in-laws are unique individuals also, and one of the greatest gifts we as a couple can give them is to allow them the freedom to express their individuality. So we give them our blessing and do not interfere in their goals and dreams.

With God to guide us and love us, we make adjustments in our routines and our way of life that accommodate our loved ones' diversity. We appreciate every member of our family and let them know that we do love and value them. We live together in an environment of love and understanding.

"Love never ends."
—1 Corinthians 13:8

Day 100

——◆——

*Through communicating with each other,
we enhance our relationship.*

**COMMUNI-
CATION**

Although it might be easy for us to blame each other for something, we know that pointing the finger of blame doesn't solve anything. So we look for ways that help us avoid the same kind of mistake in the future. In the process, we encourage better communication between us.

If one of us does something that the other disagrees with, we avoid the temptation of declaring it wrong. Instead, we listen to each other's reasons for doing what was done and understand the situation from a different perspective. More than likely, we discover that we were not aware of all that was being considered in making that decision.

Although we may not agree, we have gained insight about each other's thoughts and actions. Through communication, we have enhanced our relationship and our understanding of each other.

> "Create in me a clean heart, O God, and put
> a new and right spirit within me."
> —Psalms 51:10

Day 101

—◆—

Observing a time of rest and relaxation,
we refresh ourselves and our relationship.

REST AND RELAXATION A vacation is a wonderful way to put our busy life on hold and to enjoy both the scenery and each other. Our sharing a time of rest and relaxation is important for us. Seeing each other in a totally different environment when we vacation away from home, we find qualities we had never noticed or had forgotten.

On regular days, we might not be at home together during much of our waking hours. So when we vacation at home, we can either slow down and take it easy or combine our talents in completing some special project.

There is an ease that flows through our conversations when we are relaxed. We remember the past and plan for the future. We appreciate being with each other and especially appreciate God for bringing us together.

> "My people will abide in a peaceful habitation,
> in secure dwellings, and in quiet resting places."
> —Isaiah 32:18

Day 102

—◆—

Living in an awareness of our Creator,
we are blessed.

LIVING TODAY

This is a day for living, for being totally conscious of each other and all the great and wonderful things we can accomplish together.

Although we may dream of a bigger and better home in the future, the home we live in is the place where life is happening today! With some paint and cooperation, we are not only brightening the walls, we are also brightening the atmosphere in which we live.

God is the light of love that is constantly brightening our lives—no matter where we may be. Living in an awareness of our Creator, we are blessed. We discover new blessings that each moment brings us. Going for a walk together, we see the creative power of God at work in people and in nature. The more of life we see, the more alive we feel. And walking together is a great opportunity to hold hands.

> "So acknowledge today and take to heart
> that the Lord is God in heaven above
> and on the earth beneath; there is no other."
> —Deuteronomy 4:39

Day 103

We are in God's tender care.

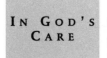

IN GOD'S CARE

There is no better place for us to be than in God's care. How reassuring it is to know that there is no place we can be that is beyond the care of God. In our home or at work, in our own neighborhood or in a place far from home, we are in God's safekeeping.

Our vital connection with God cannot be broken—not by circumstances nor distances. This is true for our family also. Whether our children are going off to kindergarten or college, whether they are in their own homes or someplace halfway around the world, they too are in God's care.

God is the presence of life and wisdom within each one of us. As precious as we are to each other and our family is to us, we know that we are all even more precious to God.

**"How precious is your steadfast love, O God!
All people may take refuge in the shadow of your wings."
—Psalms 36:7**

Day 104

———◆———

Our Prayer

Dear God,

We trust You and know that You are always with us. And that is why we know that with Your help, there is no problem we cannot work out to the satisfaction of us both.

Sometimes, God, You are our mediator, and we are so grateful when we think of how things have worked out in the past. There were times when a disagreement could have become a full-blown argument, yet something within us both told us it was a time to step back and just think about what the other person was saying.

Listening to You, God, we understand how important good communication is. It has also taught us how important it is to show our love and affection for each other and to give unconditional support. We have the confidence to step out in faith and be our true selves.

"If anyone has a complaint against another, forgive each other; just as the Lord has forgiven you." —Colossians 3:13

DAILY WORD FOR COUPLES

Day 105

—◆—

My Gift to You

I GIVE YOU THE GIFT OF MY HIGHEST REGARD.

As we continue together in life, my regard for you grows more and more. Not only do you give me the love and support I need, but you are also so loving and supportive of our other family members and our friends.

I admire your ability to be yourself in any situation, and you encourage me to do the same. Whether we are home alone or with a group of other people, you are able to express your heartfelt feelings and helpful ideas to me and to them.

I appreciate the way you always seem to put the well-being of others so high on your list of priorities. Your love for humanity and for all God's creation brings an expanded dimension to our relationship.

My prayer today and every day is that I will never forget to tell you how much I love you and how highly I regard you and all that you do.

> "God's love has been poured into our hearts
> through the Holy Spirit that has been given to us."
> —Romans 5:5

Day 106

*Each day is a new frontier—a new adventure
in living and loving for us.*

**NEW
FRONTIER**

Life is full of wonder—and how wonderful it is to share life with you. We share the same values and ideals, and we are willing to explore each new frontier together.

Each day is a new adventure—a day filled with life and love. As we move forward in life, we discover so much, and realizing this, we cannot wait to see what new wonders we will explore together.

We have so much to look forward to! We each have within us a nurturing spirit that allows us to help and cherish each other, the children in our home, and the people in our lives. On holidays or in day-to-day matters, we look for and experience a newness and wonder that take on new meaning because we are sharing them together.

Life offers us a new frontier each day—a new adventure in living and loving.

**"Surely goodness and mercy
shall follow me all the days of my life."
—Psalms 23:6**

Day 107

—◆—

*Our hearts are filled with gratitude for the joy
that we have brought to each other.*

GRATEFUL HEARTS
We are grateful for each other and feel blessed to be together. We bring joy to every day that we share and we lift each other's spirits.

Our individual strengths enhance our relationship, and we are thankful that together we can reach new heights of achievement.

Our love brings out a natural response in us to each other. Spirit to spirit, heart to heart, we are drawn together in a union of love.

Our world would not be complete without each other, and our life is much richer because we have each other.

We give thanks to God for every day. God surely has blessed us and continues to bless us in a sacred union of our grateful hearts.

> **"Now we have received not the spirit of the world,
> but the Spirit that is from God, so that we may
> understand the gifts bestowed on us by God."
> —1 Corinthians 2:12**

Day 108

—◆—

Thank God for our family and friends.

TEAMWORK   God has graced us with wonderful family and friends. These special people have helped us during some of the most trying times and celebrated with us during some of our most triumphant times.

On occasion, children have been our advisors: "Don't worry; everything will be okay." They were right. Elders have offered: "We're here to tell you that you will make it through this; we did when we were your age." And we did make it. Other times, we felt the prayers of our loved ones virtually lifting us out of fear and anxiety.

Whether they are pitching in physically to help us with some project or pitching in prayerfully to help us realize more fully the presence of God, our family and friends are important members of our team.

> "So then, whenever we have an opportunity,
> let us work for the good of all, and especially
> for those of the family of faith."
> —Galatians 6:10

Day 109

———◆———

Giving and receiving love and understanding,
we achieve balance in our relationship.

BALANCE Just as we need balance in our lives
in order to be healthy and fulfilled
individuals, we also need balance in
our relationship in order to be a
healthy and fulfilled couple. Loving, supporting, and
understanding each other bring balance to our
relationship.

Yet at times it may seem as if the one who is working
overtime or attending classes is contributing less time
and attention to our family than the other one is. Our
understanding makes it possible for us to support each
other in achieving our individual goals.

At others times, one of us is able to give more
because that one has less activity going on during a
particular day. This is okay, too, because in the long run,
our times of giving are balanced so that we both
contribute to the wholeness of our relationship.

> "Like good stewards of the manifold grace
> of God, serve one another with whatever gift
> each of you has received."
> —1 Peter 4:10

Day 110

—◆—

*The order of God supports us in experiencing life
and in developing a deeper bond with each other.*

**DIVINE
ORDER**

There is a divine order that flows throughout our life. When we first met, we knew that we were meant for each other and meant to share a lifetime together. As our relationship has grown and deepened, we have helped bring out the best in each other. We have a partnership of love.

Yet we still have more to learn about each other and about strengthening our relationship. All in accordance with divine order, God gives us what we need to know to build up our strengths as individuals and as a couple.

We have learned how good it is to share joy. We have learned how good it is to give each other love and comfort.

The order of God supports us in experiencing life and also developing a stronger bond between us as we do.

"O come, let us sing to the Lord. . . . Let us come
into his presence with thanksgiving."
—Psalms 95:1–2

Day 111

---◆---

*We are eager to give the love and understanding
that God has already prepared us to give.*

FIRST TO FORGIVE Sometimes our not being able to quickly make up after a disagreement is because we are not willing to be the first to forgive. We may believe that the first one to forgive is admitting, "I was wrong; you were right." Yet who's right and who's wrong about a simple matter can never be more important than how we treat each other.

Knowing this, we feel good about being the first one to bring an end to any contention between us. We are companions in life. God has given us more of all the love and understanding we will ever need to be forgiving.

Giving love and understanding to each other, we are helping our marriage remain strong. Now that's something we are both eager and willing to do.

**"Let us therefore no longer pass judgment
on one another, but resolve instead never to put
a stumbling block or hindrance in
the way of another."
—Romans 14:13**

Day 112

*The spirit of God guides us in being people
who love and respect each other.*

**BEING
OURSELVES**
We are thankful that we can be
ourselves and not let any pretense get
in the way of our relationship.

We feel comfortable together, for we
have allowed ourselves to know each other as we truly
are. We are kind and loving, so we know that we are
always being held in high regard by each other.

We have made a commitment to be ourselves. At one
time or another, both of us have revealed something we
wanted to improve about ourselves. We did not judge
each other; we encouraged each other to improve.

In being ourselves, we are showing how two people
in love build a life together. Most important, in being
ourselves, we are being the loving couple that God's
spirit within encourages us to be and guides us in being.

"So deeply do we care for you that we
are determined to share with you not only
the gospel of God but also our own selves, because
you have become very dear to us."
—1 Thessalonians 2:8

Day 113

—◆—

*Blending our lives, we both find fulfillment
in our relationship.*

**BLENDING
OUR
LIVES**
If we both thought only about our individual desires and needs, we would be missing out in experiencing what a relationship truly is. So we have learned to blend our lives and our needs so that we are two people who have become an integrated whole.

Happiness is a connection we share, yet it is also important that we each have our own interests. Having individual interests and activities gives us a greater appreciation of our time together and also inspires us to know that the wonderful person we fell in love with is making great strides forward in achieving meaningful accomplishments.

As time goes by, our interests may change, because we are changing. Growth and change are natural to healthy individuals and in a healthy relationship. We are growing and our love for each other is growing also.

> "We want each one of you to show the same
> diligence so as to realize the full assurance
> of hope to the very end."
> —Hebrews 6:11

Day 114

———◆———

Giving our life the light touch is looking to the light of God
to reveal whatever we need to know and to do.

LIGHT TOUCH   Giving our lives the light touch is not about acting irresponsibly during difficult situations. It is about not letting the difficult times crush our spirits.

Every person, every couple faces difficulties, for life is always asking us to grow through our experiences. Just when we think we have learned all we need to know about how to cope, something happens that offers us a brand new opportunity.

Yet, as we build ourselves up with prayer and our faith in God, we can cope. We have an outlook that enables us to see that there is light at the end of the tunnel. Giving our lives the light touch, we know that because God is always present, there is light that no amount of darkness can conceal. This is the light of God that reveals the answer to every challenge.

> "Cast our burden on the Lord,
> and he will sustain you;
> he will never permit
> the righteous to be moved."
> —Psalms 55:22

Day 115

—◆—

*Our quiet times help us individually
and help us to help each other.*

**QUIET
TIME**

We may not have always appreciated a time of quiet as much as we do now. We understand that when we are quiet and nothing is distracting us, we awaken to our own and each other's sacredness.

We have access to incredible power in that awakening, for we draw on the wisdom of God that is waiting to bring greater understanding into our lives. How refreshing it is to do nothing, absolutely nothing, except concentrate on the spirit of God. Out of that quiet time of sacred concentration comes renewal of mind and body.

We respect each other's times of being quiet. Retreating to the quiet of our souls, we are nourished and refreshed. We then can be so much more for each other and do so much more for each other. Our quiet times bless us both.

"Then they were glad because they had quiet,
and he brought them to their desired haven."
—Psalms 107:30

Day 116

---◆---

God is the source of our prosperity.

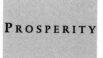

PROSPERITY

Whether at this time we are a single- or double-income family, we both recognize that we each have an important part to play concerning our finances.

When only one of us is working outside the home, we know that both of us have responsibilities to fulfill—on the job and at home. We have the highest esteem for each other's contributions to the quality of our life together. Those responsibilities may be different and they may be shared.

Whatever our circumstances may be, we know that one thing is true above all else: God is the true source of our prosperity. God is directing us in every decision we make—from increasing our income to spending it wisely. Knowing that God is the source of our supply eases tension about our finances and helps us to cope with all our responsibilities.

> "Strive for the greater gifts. And I will show you
> a still more excellent way."
> —1 Corinthians 12:31

Day 117

—◆—

*Combining our strengths and uniting with the infinite
power of God, we move forward.*

**COMBINING
OUR
STRENGTHS**
Moving ahead in life, we may have
to move several mountainlike
challenges. Whether they are of a
physical or an emotional nature, we
can do it. We will overcome them and move ahead. We
face any challenge with strength of spirit and peace of
mind, because we are able to combine our strengths and
work together to overcome any obstacles in our way.

Common sense tells us that two people tackling a
problem is better than just one person taking it on.
When it comes to working out solutions, we realize that
we are united with each other and united with the
infinite power of God. No obstacle will come between
the two of us or between God and us.

With faith in God and faith in ourselves, we can
conquer any mountain that seems to be standing
between us and our blessings.

"For truly I tell you, if you have faith the size of
a mustard seed, you will say to this mountain,
'Move from here to there,' and it will move; and nothing
will be impossible for you."—Matthew 17:20

Day 118

◆

We are following a divine pattern of life.

DIVINE PATTERN

The patterns within our lives reveal themselves in our traits, routines, and tendencies. We may need to establish new patterns in order to keep a peaceful household when our sleep or work routines are disturbed or changed.

We can because God is our source of divine ideas for establishing and following a pattern that offers us the most peace and fulfillment. In fact, God is the standard in all that we do.

As we ask ourselves and each other, "How would God have us handle this?" we may not consciously think of such a question as a prayer, but it is. This concise, simple question opens our thoughts to divine solutions.

God is showing us our path in life. Our responsibility is to be on our God-directed path.

> "You show me the path of life. In your presence there is fullness of joy; in your right hand are pleasures forevermore."
> —Psalms 16:11

Day 119

---◆---

Our Prayer

Dear God,

Words cannot begin to express the gratitude
we feel in being loving partners who are sharing
life together.

Of all Your creations, we can't help but believe
that each other is among Your greatest
achievements. We are thankful to have the
opportunity to experience true love and all its
blessings.

We feel such peace knowing that we have a
soul mate with whom we can share our thoughts
and feelings. Whatever is on our hearts and minds,
we can express it and know that we will not be
criticized, only loved and cherished.

As friends and confidants, we mean all the
world to each other. Every day is a day to give
thanks that we share our life and our innermost
thoughts. We make each day a pleasure we
experience together.

"Every day I will bless you."
—Psalms 145:2

DAILY WORD FOR COUPLES

Day 120

—◆—

My Gift to You

**I GIVE YOU THE GIFT
OF MY SENSE OF HUMOR.**

I can't explain how good I feel when I know you experience joy in being with me. We are helpmates to each other, and I think humor helps us to cope with some of life's frustrations.

So I am directing my best efforts toward sharing a sense of humor that helps us both put challenges in perspective—in their place, which is at a manageable level. I will be wise in using humor; this means that I will try to lighten the atmosphere with an upbeat attitude but never make fun of you or anyone else.

Humor helps us look on the bright side of life. We understand that challenges are temporary and that God's presence is forever with us. Knowing that we are always in God's presence is reason to feel joy.

The gladness within our souls shines out from us to brighten the dreariest of days. Sharing the gift of gladness with you increases my joy and adds meaning to my day.

"You bestow on him blessings forever; you make him glad with the joy of your presence."—Psalms 21:6

God Had a Plan

By Roger Crawford

The physical challenge I was born with affected my hands, legs, and feet: I had only two fingers on my left hand and one finger on my right hand; three toes on my left foot and a partially developed lower right leg, which was amputated when I was 5. After being fitted with an artificial leg, I was able to walk and run like other children for the first time in my life.

I am convinced that God did not waste a handicap on me. Having a handicap has taught me empathy and compassion and thankfulness. I have also learned that handicaps come in many forms—physical, emotional, intellectual, and attitudinal. There are scars on my hands and legs, but it is the invisible scars that can be infinitely more difficult to overcome.

During my growing-up years, my mother would often remind me: "Roger, it's not the gift wrapping in life that matters. What matters is the gift inside the wrapping. God gives everyone wonderful gifts—in different wrappings."

So I learned not to let what I could not do get in the way of what I could do. I started playing tennis at the age of 12 when I learned I could grip the racket by placing the one finger on my right hand between the bars of the racket. In high school, I won 47 of 53 matches, and in college, I played Division I tennis.

I may be a lousy piano player, but I have a ministry as an author and motivational speaker. I have been able to help people know that they can bounce back from hardship and thrive.

As a young boy, however, I wondered if any girl would be able to look past my hands and love me. My hands were not an obstacle to my wife, Donna, when we met. She had hired me as a motivational speaker for one of the events she was booking.

God had a great plan waiting to unfold for me as I flew from California to Louisiana. The first time I saw this stunningly beautiful woman, I fell head-over-heels in love with her. I can't say it was the same for her, but we began our relationship as good friends.

It is amazing how God works: Right after Donna and I met, I began getting more and more speaking engagements in the South, near enough to Bruston, Louisiana, that I was able to drop by and visit her. The more time I spent with her, the more I loved her. She had a wonderful zest for life with a kind, caring spirit to go with it.

When I thought that we were not going beyond being friends, I was able to relax and be myself. The first dinner Donna cooked for me was an event. She had made a casserole and put it into the oven to bake. In about 5 minutes, when it was bubbling over in the oven, Donna discovered she had turned the dial to "self-clean" instead of "bake." The door to the hot oven was locked shut.

I welcomed the opportunity to show Donna what a strong man I was by forcing the door open before the casserole caught fire. Of course the door had to be replaced, but that was the best $400 casserole I have ever eaten!

I proposed marriage to Donna at Disney World, and we were married 18 months after we met. I have a wife who loves me dearly, and my physical challenges are a nonissue in our relationship. The only issues in our marriage are ordinary ones that might occur in any marriage—for instance, my forgetting to take out the trash can be a big issue!

Donna and I are friends who became partners in life and in raising our beautiful daughter, Alexa. As my partner, Donna edits my books, coordinates all my speaking engagements, and takes care of my travel arrangements—all while honoring her commitment to being a full-time mom.

Like most children, Alexa has been one of my greatest

DAILY WORD FOR COUPLES

teachers. I believe God teaches us through the innocence and truthfulness of children. They tell us what is on their minds—whether or not we want to hear it.

One day, Alexa and I went for a swim at a local pool, and I removed my artificial leg, which I had done many times in front of Alexa. As soon as I placed the leg on the ground, Alexa turned to me and said, "Daddy, cover your leg with a towel."

Tears stung my eyes. I thought I had embarrassed my little girl, but I did manage to ask, "Why?"

"Because, Daddy, if you leave your leg in the sun, it will get very hot. When you finish swimming and put it on, it will burn you!"

I had been anticipating the negative, when my child was only trying to protect me from being hurt.

The most challenging part of our marriage is balancing family life and work. Donna and I work at keeping our priorities straight. Although I travel about a hundred days a year and continue to pursue my writing career, attending church together is a priority and so is spending time with family and friends.

Our marriage is not perfect. There are times when Donna can't stand me and vice versa. Although we have the normal ebb and flow that occurs in most marriages, we do make an effort to deal with challenge rather than to avoid or ignore it.

Donna tells me that my sense of humor makes our

DAILY WORD FOR COUPLES

marriage special. We work together, but we also laugh together. When I am away from home, she has to deal with everyday life and with crisis. That includes going to social events without me and handling emergency situations, such as when she had to rush Alexa to the hospital for stitches when she fell off her bike.

Still, we both know that we have a strength to rely on that is beyond the two of us. The presence of God is with us always—when we are together and when we are apart. And we are thankful that God had a plan for us to meet each other and to live our lives together.

Day 121

—◆—

We are reaching out to each other
in faith and love.

REACHING OUT Before we entered into this relationship, most of our decisions were about our individual needs and experiences. We relied on ourselves, not each other.

As a couple, we are learning how to reach out to each other when we are not feeling well physically or emotionally. And, as when we were single, we turn within to the spirit of God for comfort and wisdom. We also understand that we are extensions of divine love. God has united us so that we can care for and about each other.

Even during those times when we are feeling fit both emotionally and physically, we know the joy that comes from reaching out to each other with a hug or with words of love and encouragement.

In good times and in the midst of a challenge, we go within to the spirit of God and reach out to each other in love and faith.

"A glad heart makes a cheerful countenance."
—Proverbs 15:13

DAILY WORD FOR COUPLES

Day 122

— ♦ —

*The peace within our souls is reflected
in our calm and poised manner.*

**CALM
AND
POISED**

We are excited when we make a discovery about ourselves or each other that helps us both. One matter of major importance to us is that when either one of us is calm and poised, that one, whether it's you or me, helps the other to remain steady and assured. It is as if we draw peace from each other's peaceful presence. The opposite is true also: When one of us becomes agitated or upset, we can both end up in a quandary.

We are of tremendous help to each other when we remain calm. We are able to think clearly and act decisively when we are centered in the peace of God within our souls.

Dealing with a flat tire in the middle of a trip or a crying child in the middle of the night, we help each other to speak and act in loving, calm ways. We bring the peace that is within us out into the situation and bless each other.

Therefore, since we are justified by faith, we have peace
with God through our Lord Jesus Christ."
—Romans 5:1

Day 123

———◆———

*The miracle of life is being expressed
by us and by all life.*

**MIRACLE
OF LIFE**

Life is a miracle of God's creation that we could not or would not ever take for granted.

We are each a miracle of life! We see the life of God within each other being expressed as we walk. We hear the life of God within each other being expressed as we talk. We touch the miracle that we are when we hold hands.

The life of God is being expressed by us, by every person and animal, by every blade of grass and every leaf. Life is in expression everywhere.

The world we live in is meant for life, and all of nature renews itself in a continuous circle of life and living. We were meant for life. God provides us with all that we need to be fulfilled and happy. The miracle-working power of God is active in us, in our lives, and in all life.

**"In his hand is the life of every living thing
and the breath of every human being."
—Job 12:10**

Day 124

— ◆ —

Our new perspectives keep us working together
and continuing in life together.

NEW PERSPECTIVE   I appreciate that we share our own personal insights about such a broad range of matters, from our relationship to world events. Although our individual perspectives may differ, by discussing them, we help each other see things in a new light so that we welcome new possibilities into our life.

We are explorers in a world of wonder, making sure that neither of us misses some treasure of an idea or an observation. As we rely on God to guide us, we are offered incredible new vistas to consider each day.

There are always many ways of looking at a single situation and making different judgments about it; the more we cooperate with each other, however, the more we are able to accomplish together. Our new perspectives encourage us to work together and to continue in life together.

"I am about to do a new thing; now it springs forth,
do you not perceive it?"
—Isaiah 43:19

Day 125

—◆—

With faith, we know this is a day of new and wonderful experiences.

THIS IS THE DAY! Making a change in life is never easy, and we may find ourselves putting off doing something because we are uncomfortable with change. Then God gently reminds us that there is no better time than now to enrich our life.

This is the day that we turn to God for divine assurance and take charge of our life! With God strengthening us, we set aside fear and make a fresh start. We leave the past behind and step forward with assurance and faith.

This is the day that we stop daydreaming about what could be and start doing it. We are capable, confident, and filled with the mighty spirit of God! We can do all that we set out to do because God is with us throughout the journey to our goals.

This is the day that we begin a new and wonderful experience in life!

"See, now is the acceptable time."
—2 Corinthians 6:2

Day 126

$\diamond$

We are lights of love.

LIGHT OF LOVE   We are beloved companions, and it is so evident that the spirit of God within us is our source of energy and inspiration.

The love of God shines out from us as kind words and thoughtful actions that comfort and encourage us.

Although others may believe that we chose each other; we know that God brought us together. We thank God for the love and life we share.

We are lights of love that shine during our days and illumines our dreams at night. We offer sound wisdom concerning both the complex and simple decisions we face.

We are the inspiration that uplifts each other when others say there is no hope. God truly blesses us in our unity of love.

> **"It is you who light my lamp;
> the Lord, my God,
> lights up my darkness."**
> **—Psalms 18:28**

Day 127

We celebrate each of our achievements as another milestone in our relationship.

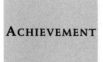

ACHIEVEMENT

The milestones we have reached together may not seem consequential to others, but each one is an important achievement for us.

Our accomplishments come in many forms—purchasing a home together, watching our family grow, and reaching another anniversary date are but a few. Each achievement is a cause for celebration and for us to give thanks to God for the blessing that each day is and for the blessing that sharing it with each other is.

We may not know exactly what is ours to do in the future, but we do know that more opportunities await us. We recognize that we are both important to God's plan and important to each other.

Being channels of God's good, we are assured that we will share many more achievements in life. Together we will grow and learn more of what we are capable of achieving.

> "For this purpose he called you . . . so that you
> may obtain the glory of our Lord."
> —2 Thessalonians 2:14

Day 128

—◆—

Aware of God, we enrich our lives
and help enrich the lives of others.

AWARE OF GOD

Parents know how important it is to be aware of their children and be interested in their lives. Understanding their children's hopes and triumphs helps parents be better parents.

We are better people in all our roles and responsibilities when we are aware of and interested in the spirit of God that is within us and within others. We understand that the power of God is at work in our life and within their lives. Then we do all we can to cooperate with the divine plan that is unfolding.

God's spirit guides and inspires us to seek not only the kind of people and situations that will enrich our life, but also those we can enrich. Following God's guidance, we are continually blessed.

Aware of God, we are aware of every opportunity to do our part in fulfilling God's plan.

> **"You were going astray like sheep,**
> **but now you have returned to the shepherd**
> **and guardian of your souls."**
> **—1 Peter 2:25**

Day 129

---◆---

God is with us every day and sustains
us on every journey.

UNEXPLORED TERRITORY Because each day is new and we are moving forward into unexplored territory, we may feel at times as if we are trying to make our way through a virtual wilderness. Even what seemed routine only yesterday can cause us to make adjustments in our thinking and activities today.

We prepare ourselves for each day of life by deciding what we will give up and what we will take with us. So let's agree to give up fear and acknowledge that the spirit of God goes with us into each new day and sustains us on every journey. We give up worrying about life—our own life and the lives of our loved ones—and call on our faith in God to uplift us.

We are living in God's presence and from our faith in God. Led by God in all that we do, we are courageous and fulfilled.

> "Jesus, full of the Holy Spirit, returned
> from the Jordan and was led by the Spirit
> in the wilderness."
> —Luke 4:1

Day 130

We are here for each other as loving companions and friends.

HERE FOR EACH OTHER

Many things in life need to be repeated. Watching a sunset or a sunrise just one time doesn't satisfy our longing to see the beauty of God's creativity. Singing just one song never allows us to experience the full range of our voices or the joy of singing.

Telling each other that we are here for each other is something we want to repeat often. We are companions and friends in the best of times and also in what seems the worst of times. We are here to uplift each other when we feel downhearted, to be with each other in observing the wonder of God every day.

When one of us is not feeling well, we know that the other one will pitch in to help or simply sit close by and hold hands.

We are here for each other now and always.

> "Where you go, I will go; where you lodge,
> I will lodge; your people shall be my people,
> and your God my God."
> —Ruth 1:16

Day 131

—◆—

*In large and small ways, we contribute
to each other's personal growth.*

**PERSONAL
GROWTH**

We have grown as a couple, learning what it takes to make our relationship one in which we both are fulfilled. We have also grown as individuals in our family roles and in our careers. Although we have learned much on our own and together, God was the one who directed us in gaining greater knowledge and helped us to interpret all through a spirit-filled mind.

We are mates and helpers taking pride in what each other has accomplished. When one of us has had to spend more time than usual away from home, the other was there to fill in for the one who was away. In large and small ways, we have contributed to each other's personal growth.

Our caring about and for each other gives us each a monumental boost of courage and determination.

"I planted, Apollos watered,
but God gave the growth."
—1 Corinthians 3:6

Day 132

❖

Our gentle reminders to each other bless us both.

GENTLE REMINDERS

With all of the information we are continually adding to our store of memories, it is only natural that occasionally we may need a gentle reminder of something.

When we leave each other a note or call to remind each other of something, we are acting from a loving, caring attitude. We never want to give the impression that we do not trust each other's memory. Sometimes a reminder is something we both need to keep something fresh in our memories.

We welcome gentle reminders. Every day we have telephone numbers, appointment times, and much more that we need to remember. A reminder from one of us can be just what the other needs to keep on schedule.

Offering reminders is just one way of expressing our love. Gentle reminders are given and accepted as gestures of a loving, caring couple.

"Those who counsel peace have joy."
—Proverbs 12:20

DAILY WORD FOR COUPLES

Day 133

---◆---

*We share our home and the space in our home
in courteous, thoughtful ways.*

**SHARING
SPACE**

If every day or even most days we lived our life at a leisurely pace, we would have fewer annoyances and aggravations to deal with. If only . . . But the reality is that many times we are so busy rushing around the house to get ready for work or to be on time for an appointment that we may get in each other's way.

We share a home and that means we share space in our home. This may not be as easy to do as it sounds, but because we are committed to each other, we cooperate in simple matters that might otherwise turn into a major problem when we are in a hurry. We are courteous to and thoughtful of each other.

God has blessed us abundantly, and there are so many ways that we can bless each other. Sharing the space in our home is a simple but important one.

"And God is able to provide you with every blessing
in abundance, so that by always having enough
of everything, you may share abundantly in
every good work."—2 Corinthians 9:8

Day 134

—◆—

Our Prayer

Dear God,

What relief we feel as our whole bodies respond to our thoughts! We relax as we think about lying in the warm sand of a secluded beach.

We relax also when we think about healing. We know that Your spirit of life is the source of all the healing we could ever need, a constant flow of energy and renewal within us and through us.

With every thought of You and prayer to You, we are answering *yes* to the presence of Your healing life and opening the door to hope and renewal.

In prayer, God, we are doing something positive for ourselves and our other loved ones. Our thoughts and words are of life and healing, for they spring forth from Your presence within. Your life is expressing health and well-being through us today and always.

> "My child, be attentive to my words. . . .
> For they are life to those who find them,
> and healing to all their flesh."
> —Proverbs 4:20, 22

Day 135

—◆—

My Gift to You

I GIVE YOU THE GIFT OF MY UNDERSTANDING.

When I say good night to you, I silently give thanks to God for you and give thanks that our relationship is one of love.

Maintaining our relationship calls for the investment of our time and attention. So I am giving you the gift of my understanding. This means that I am willing to listen to all that you have to tell me. I act as your sounding board as you recap the events of the day or as you express your feelings about a challenge.

I understand that some of the stress and discomfort you are feeling will be reflected in what you say, but you are not angry with me. I remain understanding— confident enough that our love for each other will enable us to withstand the challenge.

I do what I can to ensure that when we say good night and close our eyes, the very atmosphere around us is filled with love and understanding.

"May the Lord direct your hearts to the love of God
and to the steadfastness of Christ."
—2 Thessalonians 3:5

Day 136

—◆—

*We follow the Golden Rule, a sacred guideline
for giving and receiving blessings.*

**THE
GOLDEN
RULE**
The positive, basic guidelines we learned as children about being polite, taking turns, and being fair helped us get along with others. These guidelines are just as useful to us today.

The foundation of these guidelines is the Golden Rule. Giving others the same reverence, kindness, and love that we want others to give us leaves no room for doubt about what is the right thing to do or to say.

The Golden Rule is a sacred guideline that we follow, and it has been a tremendous blessing to us, allowing us to move past petty feelings and any urge to repay one slight with an even greater one. Using the Golden Rule brings our thoughts and actions back to the basics of love and kindness, respect and compassion. What a pleasure it is to give the blessings that this sacred guideline inspires us to give.

> **"In everything do to others as you
> would have them do to you."**
> **—Matthew 7:12**

DAILY WORD FOR COUPLES

Day 137

—◆—

We use stepping-stones of understanding, patience, and consideration in honoring our relationship.

STEPPING-STONES If we were walking on a trail and came to a small stream of water, we hopefully would find stepping-stones that would allow us to cross to the other side—safe and dry.

At times, we may come to a seeming impasse in our relationship also, but using stepping-stones of prayer, understanding, and patience, we reach a resolution.

We are considerate of each other's feelings and thoughts as we express our own. Being honest with ourselves and each other, we recognize that each of our ideas has merit. Or we understand that a solution may be a combination of our ideas. We are open to all possibilities.

Our individual ways may not be the best. Our united way may be better, for we have used stepping-stones of understanding, patience, and consideration in honoring our relationship.

"Not that I have already obtained this or have already reached the goal; but I press on to make it my own."
—Philippians 3:12

Day 138

— ◆ —

*Alert to divine ideas, we actively participate
in a divine plan.*

**DIVINE
IDEAS**

Even when we believe a decision is right for us, we may hesitate following through with it. The reason could be that we sense that God is revealing the best plan for carrying out that decision. God is asking for our attention, and we give it.

We give our attention to God by listening in prayer. Alert to divine ideas, we will not rush into new situations. As we make a job change or travel in unfamiliar places, we feel such peace of mind.

The powerful benefits of our prayer times are reflected in our life. We are able to go about doing the things we need to do with confidence. We approach both opportunities and challenges knowing that God is our guide and our inspiration.

There is a divine plan unfolding in our life, and we are open and receptive to it.

"The Lord will guide you continually."
—Isaiah 58:11

Day 139

$\diamond$

*We learn from experiencing
the presence of God.*

**DIVINE
PRESENCE**

Our experiences in life continue to be some of our greatest opportunities to learn. From both our successes and mistakes, we learn what works for us.

In the process, we discover positive ways to interact with family, friends, and each other. Yet the most important thing we realize is that we learn the most from experiencing the presence of God in *every* experience.

Communing with God, we receive divine wisdom. Even if the guidance we receive is not what we had envisioned, we accept it. We know that perhaps the decision we would have made on our own would not have allowed a blessing to happen to us and through us.

Experiencing the presence of God teaches us that the greatest knowledge comes from within the soul, where God and we are one.

**"And there will be no more night; they need no light
of lamp or sun, for the Lord God will be their light."
—Revelation 22:5**

Day 140

---◆---

We give a tender and compassionate touch
in caring for our loved ones.

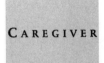

CAREGIVER

The tender touch of a caregiver soothes physical pain; it also eases the emotional pain of the one who needs comfort.

Because we care about others, we are caregivers. Whether we are caring for children or adult family members, we pray that our hands always give a gentle touch. We pray that our voices are enriched with love and compassion as we talk. We pray that our thoughts are uplifted with ideas that promote life, love, and understanding.

We also include in our prayers the health care professionals who help all members of our family stay healthy and fit. They are loving caregivers when our health is challenged. Their kind and caring ways are important in helping us regain our health and vitality.

"A Samaritan while traveling came near him; and when he saw him, he was moved with pity. He went to him and bandaged his wounds. . . . Then he put him on his own animal, brought him to an inn, and took care of him."
—Luke 10:33–34

Day 141

◆

*Our strategies for living
begin with prayer.*

STRATEGIES
FOR LIVING
Strategies for living may sound too
much like a scientific approach to
everyday life. Yet a strategy is simply a
carefully thought out plan. What better
plan could we have than to allow God to lead us in
making all other plans.

It's true; we don't know what the future holds. We
do know that in order to buy a bigger house, send our
children to college, and retire, we need to have some
kind of plan that has been prayerfully considered.

All strategies are not about long-term matters. The
different activities of our family today may call for quick
strategy. For instance, we can't be in two places at one
time, but we can plan so that one of us drives our
children to their events, while the other takes a family
member to the doctor. Then we both still keep our own
schedules.

Prayer always prepares us to make the best plans.

**"Prepare your work outside, get everything ready for you
in the field; and after that build your house."
—Proverbs 24:27**

Day 142

—◆—

Through the power and presence of God's spirit,
we are resilient!

RESILIENT SPIRIT

We have learned that each day presents its own set of opportunities and challenges. Life is happening every day. Because we have a resilient spirit, we perceive what is happening as an opportunity rather than a challenge. Then we are able to achieve what we have never before achieved.

We can and do rise to every occasion with faith, because God is the very spirit of life and wisdom that enlivens us and encourages us to move forward. We dare to hope that each day unfolds in order and that any seeming disorder is dissolved as we apply spiritual principles in everyday living and in a crisis.

You and I have a resilient spirit that enables us to remain positive when things appear to be going wrong. As we watch and pray, as we hold to our faith and love of life, we will overcome challenge and accept every opportunity to express life, love, and understanding.

"A new heart I will give you, and a new spirit
I will put within you."
—Ezekiel 36:26

Day 143

◆

*Letting God love through us, we are learning
to love each other unconditionally.*

**LOVING
UNCONDI-
TIONALLY**
It takes courage for us to love each
other without reservation. Yet when
we consider the depth of the love we
have for each other, it is not difficult
for either of us to love the other unconditionally.

Consciously, we would never withhold love until it
was earned, because we know the joy that loving brings
us. At one time we may have believed or been taught
that only God can love unconditionally. God's grace is
the assurance that we can never do or say anything that
would cause God to withhold love. Still there may be
times when we forget to follow God's example of love.

We strive to love unconditionally, and God is helping
us along our way. God loves us both, and letting God
love through us, we are learning to love unconditionally.

"Love one another. Just as I have loved you,
you also should love one another."
—John 13:34

Day 144

—◆—

God is our constant companion.

SACRED COMPANION As we pray, each time we pray, we are fortified with strength and courage. Aware that we are enfolded in God's loving presence, we realize that no matter where we may go—whether we travel together or separately—God is with us. Always, you and I are united by the spirit of God.

We may not know what today or even the next moment holds in store for us; we do know, however, that God is our constant companion. God is with us to uplift us when we become disappointed and to guide us in making decisions.

Blessed by God's guidance, we express our thoughts clearly to each other and know that the plans we make are right for us. When we are at work or at home, when we walk in our own neighborhood or travel miles away, God is our companion.

"David said further to his son Solomon, 'Be strong
and of good courage, and act. Do not be afraid
or dismayed; for the Lord God, my God, is with you.' "
—1 Chronicles 28:20

DAILY WORD FOR COUPLES

Day 145

—◆—

*Our family is a treasure of love
that we share.*

**OUR
FAMILY**

Coming together as a family has presented us with many more fulfilling experiences than trying ones. Our life has been an unfolding saga of love and acceptance that brought together several people into one household. What were yours and mine has become ours.

Such an adjustment in our thinking about material things and family members didn't happen immediately. Yet it did happen. The love in our hearts and our dedication to being a family have united us day by day, year by year.

We are a family, united by God's love and our commitment to love each other. Everyone and everything in our home is ours. Our family is a treasure of love that we share.

"Clap your hands, all you peoples; shout to God
with loud songs of joy. For the Lord, the Most High,
is awesome. . . . He chose our heritage for us."
—Psalms 47:1–4

Day 146

—◆—

With hearts of love,
we say, "I love you!"

**SAYING
"I LOVE
YOU"**
The words *I love you* may seem overused by some, but when we speak them to each other, we say them with all the conviction of our hearts. In our words of love, we want each other to hear the strength of our commitment and to be comforted by how much we care.

Our love may not be a tangible gift, but it is a source of powerful support for each other. The power in love strengthens us so that we believe the two of us can overcome any situation. Our love for God and for each other fills us with a joy that can never be extinguished. When all is said and done, we rely on love to guide us through.

We want to give 100 percent in all that we do with each other. We do so with joy in our hearts, because we are saying the words *I love you* to someone incredibly wonderful.

> **"All the paths of the Lord
> are steadfast love and faithfulness."**
> **—Psalms 25:10**

Day 147

---◆---

Together we share a vision of good.

VISION OF GOOD

In talking about our future, we are sharing a vision of good for things to come. Our dreams are filled with hope because we know that God is now and will be forever at the core of our beings and at the center of every experience in our life.

If we seem to lack motivation, it may be because we are caught up in our everyday routines. So let's remember that God never has and never will limit our opportunities to use our imagination to dream and our ability to follow our dreams. We break free from the routine of life by accepting life for the blessing that it is.

We encourage each other to recognize the blessings we have and to envision the unlimited blessings before us. In our vision of good, we include our loved ones. Looking to what lies ahead, we know we will be sharing a love of God and each other, a love of family and friends.

> **"Happy are those whose strength is in you,
> in whose heart are the highways to Zion."**
> **—Psalms 84:5**

Day 148

◆

*One in spirit, we share
a sacred connection.*

**ONE
IN SPIRIT**

We have heard about and have
known couples that have connected so
completely in heart and soul that they
anticipated each other's thoughts and
needs without a word being spoken.

We, too, are keeping a sacred connection between us,
a oneness in spirit, by not only listening to each other
but also doing our best to understand each other.

Having given our time and attention to each other,
we know at a glance the thought behind even the
slightest expression. One in spirit, we sense each other's
need for help or need not to be interrupted for a while.

Keeping all ways of communicating active is
important to us, and the intuitive knowing that we
share is an added blessing that comes from the spirit of
God within us.

> **"It is right for me to think this way
> about all of you, because you hold me
> in your heart."**
> **—Philippians 1:7**

Day 149

---◆---

Our Prayer

Dear God,

Today, we are uniting our hearts in a time of prayer. You are the presence of peace that pervades our days and nights, and infuses our relationship with love and understanding. It is very clear that we could not make our relationship as loving and fulfilling on our own. Thank You for guiding us and loving us.

Because You are the heart in our relationship, we do love each other with a love that honors You and blesses us. We are a couple that knows the importance of building a life of prayer together. We are in touch with the love and peace within our souls so that we relate to each other in compassionate and helpful ways.

Centering ourselves in an awareness of Your presence, we recognize that we are spiritual beings. We also are aware of the loving and tender ways that we can express our humanness to each other.

**"We, for our part, will devote ourselves
to prayer and to serving the word."**
—Acts 6:4

DAILY WORD FOR COUPLES

Day 150

—◆—

My Gift to You

I GIVE YOU THE GIFT OF MY REDISCOVERIES.

Sometimes I am so busy that I don't take time to enjoy the beauty and wonder that God has created. Then I remember to look at the world from a faith-filled perspective and rediscover the glory of God all around me.

Today I give you the gift of my rediscoveries:

I was reminded of what a wonderful example of an I-can attitude an ant offers when I saw a tiny ant lifting an object that was several times bigger than it was.

Every time I share from the heart and soul, I rediscover how good it feels to let the spirit of God express love and understanding through me to you.

With each and every prayer, we are rediscovering our own spirituality. Living as divinely inspired creations of God, we give so much to each other. I know that each day I am rediscovering how blessed I am being with you.

"Every generous act of giving, with every perfect gift, is from above, coming down from the Father of lights, with whom there is no variation or shadow due to change."
—James 1:17

GOD WILL GET US THROUGH

BY DELILAH

In 1994, my husband, Doug, and I and our son, Isaiah, were living in Pennsylvania where I was a DJ at a local radio station. Doug was working toward a degree at the local college, and I was due to deliver our new baby in 2 months. I loved our life—my job, our home, and the neighborhood where we lived.

Then the radio station where I worked changed formats, and I was laid off. Doug and I prayed, and I sent out résumés and tapes to other stations in the area, but nothing happened.

After a while, with still no job prospects, Doug came to me and said, "I feel that God is leading us back to Massachusetts."

My immediate reply was: "Absolutely not! I am not going back there!"

Doug and I had met in Massachusetts and lived there awhile, but some really unpleasant things had happened with a group of people I thought were our friends. I was also resistant to the move because I was afraid my in-laws would be a bit too close and overprotective of my husband. So I kept saying: "I'm not going back there. God would not take me back there. He just wouldn't do that to me!" But Doug was sure that this was what God wanted us to do.

I was really angry—angry at God, angry at the station that had let me go. I felt that God didn't care about me or my needs. I went to bed one night filled with all this anger, and when I woke up the next morning, I was unable to move. I had to be helped out of bed to go to the doctor's office. There we learned that the baby's head was lodged in my pelvic region—right up against my sciatic nerve.

I was literally a cripple. This condition continued for days, and I was in so much pain. One evening I prayed as I was soaking in the tub to relieve the pain, and God really spoke to my heart: "Do you want to wrestle with Me like Jacob did?" I started crying, and in complete surrender, I said, "Okay, God, whatever You want, I'll do." I got up out of the tub, and the pain was completely gone.

Doug and I made plans to move back to Massachusetts—back to the house we still owned there, back to the neighborhood I did not want to return to. I was filled with fear about finding a new job, but I had told God I would go back. So we did after our daughter, Shaylah, was born.

Six weeks after we moved and I started a new job, my mother was diagnosed with terminal cancer. She lived in Oregon, so my sister and I took turns flying out there to care for her before and after her surgery. After getting Mom settled in with home health care, I returned to Massachusetts expecting to lose my job. Looking back, I can see how God's plan for us to be in Massachusetts was perfect. My general manager told me to take as much time off as I needed, and I never missed a paycheck. He was very compassionate, in part because his mother had had brain cancer.

My in-laws took wonderful care of my son and my husband while I was gone—making sure they were fed and had clean clothes. I took Shaylah with me, and we were gone off and on for 9 months before Mom passed away.

Three months later I was again laid off because of a change in formats, but I put my trust in God. I put my fears aside and knew in my heart that when the time was right, God would open a door for me. Soon after that, I had an opportunity to go into syndication with my own radio show.

I've learned through my life's experiences to pray about everything—from a car that won't start to a healing need. When I have to make public appearances, I pray for the

DAILY WORD FOR COUPLES

right words to say. Some people believe that prayer is only for times of crisis—when a loved one is dying or the bank is foreclosing on the family home. But I believe that God is interested in and cares about even the smallest details of our lives.

Nothing is too difficult for God. No matter what we are going through—a difficult move, the loss of a loved one, or a painful divorce—if we can just hold on to our faith in God, God will get us through it.

Day 151

—◆—

*We have faith that the spirit of God
is expressing greatness through us.*

FAITH

We have met with obstacles as we
have traveled the road of life. Keeping
faith, we have worked together to
overcome doubt.

Looking back, we now recognize that even during
those times when we were in doubt, we were not
questioning the power of God. Rather, we were
questioning our confidence in ourselves.

Experiencing what God can accomplish through us
and observing what God can accomplish through
others increase our faith. Faith continues to build us up
spiritually, physically, and emotionally.

We have faith in God to guide us, to love us, to keep
us safe. Our faith is founded on the power and
greatness of God. The spirit of God within us is
expressing greatness through us.

**"Out of the believer's heart
shall flow rivers of living water."**
—John 7:38

Day 152

◆

Knowing that the spirit of God lives within us,
we have a positive self-image.

SELF-IMAGE Perhaps our self-images have been damaged by things that happened to us as far back as our childhood. We can help heal our self-images by reminding ourselves of who we are: We are creations of the Creator of all that has ever been, is now, or will ever be.

We can be free from the pain of the past. Knowing that the spirit of God lives within us, we can overcome whatever it was in the past that caused us physical or emotional pain.

We understand how good it is to be who we are: God's wonderful creations. Experiencing the spirit of God within us is more than reason enough to have a positive self-image.

"What are human beings that you are mindful
of them, mortals that you care for them?
Yet you have made them a little lower than God,
and crowned them with glory and honor."
—Psalms 8:4–5

Day 153

---◆---

We are shining examples
of God's love in action!

SHINING EXAMPLES We are dedicating ourselves—in all that we are and all that we do—to being shining examples of God's love.

With such dedication, we can be the love of God expressed in our home, our workplace, and our community. God inspires us to love unconditionally, and when we act on divine inspiration, we love for the pure joy of loving, with no thought of return.

Because we are shining examples of divine love in action, we know that there are unlimited ways to give love. For example, the love that we feel flows out to each other through our conversations and through our willingness to be of help.

God loves us, and God's love is within us. Sharing the love of God with each other and with others is an added blessing in our life.

> "I will greatly rejoice in the Lord,
> my whole being shall exult in my God."
> —Isaiah 61:10

Day 154

—◆—

*We experience absolute fulfillment
knowing that we are in God's presence.*

IN GOD'S PRESENCE During our early years, we couldn't wait to grow up so that we could pass our driver's tests or move out on our own. Even now, we may be hurrying life along by looking forward to some life-changing event, such as a promotion or retirement.

Anticipation of what we have yet to experience sweetens the present, yet we don't want to miss out on the wonder of each moment by projecting our happiness and fulfillment into the future.

Some of the greatest times of our life have been in working together toward a goal, supporting and encouraging each other along the way. We have been challenged, but we have met the challenge because God is always with us. Nothing, absolutely nothing, could be more fulfilling than knowing we are in God's presence.

> "The Lord is my rock, my fortress,
> and my deliverer."
> —Psalms 18:2

Day 155

We are enthusiastic about life!

ENTHUSIASTIC

Let's thank God for this wonderful day! No matter what the weather may be—rain or shine—we will feel the blessing of every moment. No matter what situations may arise, we will experience the joy of living because we are alive with the life of God!

Our enthusiasm is born of our faith in God. When we consider the golden opportunities that each day offers, we are filled with joy—from the tops of our heads to the tips of our toes.

Enthusiasm is a wonderful motivation for us in giving our all in all that we do. When we are enthusiastic about doing something, we are charged with energy and filled with a zest for living.

The spirit of God within us is a wellspring of enthusiasm. We have all the enthusiasm we need to make our day fantastic in every way.

> **"O Lord my God, I will give thanks to you forever."**
> **—Psalms 30:12**

Day 156

— ◆ —

God is the source of all our blessings.

FINANCES There may be several things we can
do to improve our financial situation:
We may decide to take classes that will
enhance our knowledge so that we
qualify for promotions, or maybe we will have the
opportunity to turn a hobby into a moneymaking
project.

Our success in any endeavor is greatly determined by
our willingness not only to listen to divine guidance, but
also to follow through by applying it in everyday life.

Giving thanks to God as the source of all our
blessings gives a boost to our awareness of prosperity.
Expressing our appreciation to God reminds us of
blessings that we may have overlooked. Family, friends,
a comfortable home—all are blessings that make our life
complete.

"Now to him who by the power at work
within us is able to accomplish abundantly far more
than all we can ask or imagine, to him be glory."
—Ephesians 3:20–21

Day 157

—◆—

With what we do now, we can have a positive impact on today and on the future.

DIVINE APPOINTMENT

Much of what we do in life may not seem monumental or appear to have a lasting effect. Yet our being here at this time and place is a divine appointment.

We are God's ambassadors of love as we interact with each other. For instance, letting one another know how much we appreciate each other may be just what we need to hear at a particular time. With a few kind words, either one of us can help the other shift the outlook from glum to glad. The love and caring we express in a few seconds can have a lasting, positive effect on our partnership.

The tree that we plant today will have a positive effect from this time on, for it will offer beauty and shade for generations to come. Even with the simplest things we do, we can make a positive impact on today and on the future.

"Just as it is bearing fruit and growing in the whole world, so it has been bearing fruit among yourselves from the day you heard it and truly comprehended the grace of God."
—Colossians 1:6

Day 158

—◆—

As children of God, we are ageless
and eternal beings of life.

AGELESS AND ETERNAL

We are both children of God, and because we live our lives as the children of God that we truly are, we do not let age or circumstance limit us. We are ageless and eternal beings. The spirit of God renews our bodies and refreshes our minds.

Knowing our oneness with the spirit of God, we also know that we are able to overcome any doubt about our ability to accomplish something. We are capable of planning what is worthwhile to us and we are able to achieve success.

As God's beloved creations, we have energy to express and life to experience. So we do! As we embrace each opportunity to give expression to life and to experience life, we give thanks for the potential within each new day.

"Those who drink of the water that I will give them will never be thirsty. The water that I will give will become in them a spring of water gushing up to eternal life."
—John 4:14

DAILY WORD FOR COUPLES

Day 159

—◆—

The sweet mystery of God is everywhere!

SWEET MYSTERY   Life itself is such a miracle that we do not need a momentous happening to realize that God's power is at work in our life and in the universe.

We may never know all that the power of God encompasses or all that God is capable of doing. The beauty of being cared for by God is that we do not have to know the answers to these questions in order to live our life fully and completely.

The sweet mystery of God runs through all life, so there is no need for us to worry. We have faith in God concerning not only ourselves, but the rest of our family also. We face the unknown with confidence and peace of mind.

God is everywhere, and the power of God is actively renewing and restoring all!

> "Blessed be the name of God from age to age,
> for wisdom and power are his."
> —Daniel 2:20

Day 160

— ◆ —

Trusting God is essential in our plan of taking care of ourselves, each other, and our loved ones.

TAKING CARE
Because we care, we do what we can for each other and for our loved ones. Every day, we remember to include each other and family and friends in our prayers.

We also remember to care about and for ourselves. When we are feeling our best and doing our best, we share a feeling of fulfillment and we bless each other.

What do we need to do to improve and maintain our health and well-being? Eating nutritious food, exercising regularly, and getting plenty of rest all fit into our plan for healthy living. Enriching our spiritual life through prayer and meditation also enhances us emotionally and physically.

Trusting in God is a great stress reliever, and we do trust God in all matters. We are at peace because we know that God's love enfolds us.

> "All who believed were together
> and had all things in common."
> —Acts 2:44

Day 161

---◆---

*Love is the way we live and work
in harmony with each other.*

HARMONY

We both feel the tension in the air
and in our bodies when there has been
a misunderstanding or a confrontation
between us.

Then what relief we feel when our expressions of
love for each other bring harmony into the situation.

We can always find something to love in each other,
because the presence of God is within us! In even the
most difficult times, we love and respect each other.
Being aware of God's presence within us and within
each other helps us be a peaceful, harmonious couple,
no matter what is happening between us and what is
going on around us.

God is love, and the love of God inspires us to live
and work in harmony. What a blessing harmony is to us
and to those with whom we share our life.

> **"May the God of steadfastness
> and encouragement grant you to live
> in harmony with one another."
> —Romans 15:5**

Day 162

---◆---

*We release the past and move forward
into a new and brighter day.*

**BRIGHTER
DAY**

Releasing the past can be such a freeing experience for us—we no longer feel the burden of painful emotions or memories. Instead, we are free to live in the present and know we are creating bright, new memories that will bless us for a lifetime.

Free of the past, we are ready for new experiences. We are eager to reach out to life and to give back to life using the talents and abilities with which God has blessed us.

If we have talked about starting a new project or pursuing a goal, now is the time for us to make plans and to get started. We may have questions, but we are open to the answers that God will provide us with as we move forward together.

> **"The human mind plans the way,
> but the Lord directs the steps."
> —Proverbs 16:9**

Day 163

◆

Experiencing the presence of God in all
and throughout all is a joy.

 **SPIRITUAL DISCOVERY** We can imagine what the first astronauts felt while being rocketed into space. More than likely, they experienced many different human emotions.

We can imagine what these pioneers in outer space experienced when they looked down and saw planet Earth: joy in viewing the world with no boundaries and as the home of God's family.

There is joy in spiritual discovery. Each time we see ourselves or another person as a spiritual being, we are beholding the presence of God. This is an awesome experience that brings joy to our hearts and into our life.

An awareness of God is a joy that is full of glory. Being totally aware of God is being totally immersed in the presence of God. What greater joy could there be?

"My lips will shout for joy
when I sing praises to you."
—Psalms 71:23

Day 164

Our Prayer

Dear God,

We trust in You to guide us because You are God, our creator and sustainer.

We feel Your guidance as a gentle urging within our souls, as a surge of inspiration during silent prayer, or as a realization of a divine idea in the midst of activity.

We can never be away from Your loving and wise presence. So we lift ourselves up to You and know there is an answer to every prayer. That answer is a way for us to make it through the day or through a challenge.

The answer that You give is not about what we alone must do. Divine guidance assures us of all that You can do, and we have dedicated ourselves to letting Your spirit express wisdom, life, and love through us.

"If I take the wings of the morning and settle at the farthest limits of the sea, even there your hand shall lead me, and your right hand shall hold me fast."
—Psalms 139:9–10

Day 165

◆

My Gift to You

**I GIVE YOU THE GIFT
OF MY PRAYERS.**

I am praying for you, giving you a gift that flows
from the spirit of God within me. Yes, prayer is a gift
from my soul.

I thank God for you. You enrich my life, and I pray
that I always enrich your life. I pray that you are aware
of my love for you and, more important, that you are
aware of God's loving, healing presence.

My heart goes out to you in prayer. Whenever you
are going through a challenge, I want to be of help in
every way I can. I know, however, that in your greatest
times of challenge and joy, God is with you to give you
the love and understanding that only God can give.

In prayer, I experience a unity of spirit with God and
with you. In giving you the gift of my prayers, I have
peace of mind about you.

> "For with you is the fountain of life;
> in your light we see light."
> —Psalms 36:9

Day 166

—◆—

*We appreciate each other for brightening
our life and our world.*

**APPRECIATE
EACH
OTHER!**
What a joy it is for us to acknowledge each other for all that we have contributed to the quality of our life and the lives of our family. We appreciate thoughtful words and acts. Day after day, we bring sunlight into each other's day.

How do we acknowledge our appreciation? We say, "I appreciate you!" or write a note of appreciation or give each other an unexpected call when we are apart. Our message to each other may be, "I love telling you how much I appreciate you," or "Thank you for being a light of God, shining brightly in my life!"

The more we appreciate each other, the more we find to appreciate. Showing our appreciation acknowledges our best qualities and encourages us to let them come forward.

"All who see them shall acknowledge that they
are a people whom the Lord has blessed."
—Isaiah 61:9

DAILY WORD FOR COUPLES

Day 167

—◆—

God is our light, our hope, our all.

REVEALING LIGHT
In the midst of a crisis, we may feel overwhelmed. We even may question whether there is any hope, any way out.

Surely Jesus had doubt as He cried out to God, "Why have you forsaken me?" (Matthew 27:46; Mark 15:34) Then, with a surge of spiritual understanding and faith, Jesus declared, "Father, into your hands I commend my spirit." (Luke 23:46)

We, too, turn our life over to God and know that with God every crisis and every challenge will be resolved. Keeping our faith in God recharges our spiritual batteries and shines new light—divine light—onto every situation.

God is mightier than any circumstance, and divine light reveals what we need to know and do to walk our path in life.

> "He grew strong in his faith as he gave glory
> to God, being fully convinced that God was able
> to do what he had promised."
> —Romans 4:20–21

Day 168

— ◆ —

*As spiritual beings, we are creations
of beauty and majesty.*

**LOOK
WITHIN**
Let's remind each other not to
become so focused on what is
happening to us and around us that we
forget to consider what is happening
within us, at the depths of our hearts and souls.

When we do look within in a quiet time of prayer
and meditation, this is what we perceive: The spirit of
God is there sustaining and nourishing us. We behold
the beauty and majesty of spiritual beings that are more
than capable of rising above everyday concerns.

As beloved children of God, we know that there is so
much more to us than just our minds and bodies. We
are unique and awe-inspiring creations of the Creator of
all life—beings of beauty and light that reflect the spirit
of God back into the world.

"The Lord does not see as mortals see;
they look on the outward appearance,
but the Lord looks on the heart."
—1 Samuel 16:7

Day 169

———◆———

Thank God for the freedom
to overcome any limitation.

FREE

We have a sacred responsibility to take care of ourselves, and we honor that responsibility by ending any and all negative habits we have acquired.

Now is the time for us to take authority over habits instead of letting them have authority over us. God is our authority. We have the strength of mind and body that we need to overcome negative habits. We release them through the freeing power of God.

With faith in God, we will overcome anything that would try to keep us from living our freedom—every day and in every way!

Thank God that we are free! With this freedom, we focus on doing the things that are beneficial to our health and to the well-being of our relationship. Moving forward, we leave old habits behind.

> "Now the Lord is the Spirit, and where
> the Spirit of the Lord is, there is freedom."
> —2 Corinthians 3:17

Day 170

—◆—

Great is the presence of God within us!

**G O D
I S   G R E A T**   As we share a quiet moment of contemplation, we give thanks for God's creativity. When we perceive the mastery of God's creativity in all people and all places, we step into a panorama that is teeming with life and energy. No person is a stranger, no location is foreign, nothing is impossible.

Yet our faith in God does not rely on the things we are able to sense in the world. Our faith is built on our daily communion with God. As we open our hearts and souls to God, we are inviting healing, revealing responses to resound throughout our bodies, and they do.

Great are God's works, and oh, so great is God's presence in all creation. As examples of God's creativity, we are aware of God as life and understanding, as healing and renewal, as love and acceptance.

> "Great are the works of the Lord,
> studied by all who delight in them."
> —Psalms 111:2

Day 171

Intuition is the wisdom of our hearts revealing the wisdom of God to us.

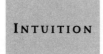

INTUITION

In praying together about a question that is on our hearts and minds, how do we know that the answer we receive is from God? We know because intuition, a wisdom of the heart, connects us with the wisdom of God.

Intuition is an inner knowing, a message of guidance that God gives to us so that we have the understanding we need to work through even the most complicated situations life can offer. We know what to say and do, and we also know what to refrain from saying and doing.

The wisdom of our hearts reveals guidance from God. Intuition, that gentle nudge from God, awakens us to a world of possibilities and reminds us that God is working through us to create a wonder-filled life.

> "Even though you do not believe me, believe the works, so that you may know and understand that the Father is in me and I am in the Father."
> —John 10:38

Day 172

— ◆ —

*Every day, we are making
a positive investment in life.*

**DAILY
INVESTMENT**

Taking care of a toddler requires a huge investment of time and patience. Yet years down the road, we may look back on such a time with longing, for we learned so much about life, love, and enthusiasm from the time we invested in children.

Each day may offer us different kinds of challenges and rewards. Then we move on to another day, knowing that we never have to go through any situation alone.

Life is change, and God is our refuge and strength in challenge and in achievement. When we accept that each day offers us opportunities to experience change and new circumstances, challenges no longer seem as challenging.

Living fully in the moment with God, we enjoy life and make a positive investment in life by doing our best—every day.

"You did not choose me but I chose you.
And I appointed you to go and bear fruit, fruit that
will last, so that the Father will give you whatever
you ask him in my name."—John 15:16

DAILY WORD FOR COUPLES

Day 173

—◆—

Giving expression to the love of God within,
we are loving and compassionate.

EXPRESSION OF LOVE Our love for each other gives us a sense of quiet strength. Love fills us with caring and compassion.

As we pray with each other and for each other, we envision our highest good, a sacred vision that blesses both of us because our lives are intertwined. Knowing that each of us is healthy and fulfilled gives both of us such joy!

We have the courage and faith to never let anything get in the way of our being a loving presence to each other. With each kind act, we are expressing love for each other.

We pray that we are blessing each other and that we add joy and meaning to whatever we experience together. Giving expression to the love of God within us, we are naturally loving and compassionate toward each other.

> "I have said these things to you
> so that my joy may be in you, and
> that your joy may be complete."
> —John 15:11

Day 174

_Our relationship with God enhances our relationship
with each other._

**BEING
A COUPLE**

We agree that it takes the two of
us to form our relationship. Yet we
know that it is our relationship with
God that blesses our relationship
with each other.

Knowing that God's spirit is present within us
reminds us that we honor each other through a sacred,
committed relationship. When we each bring spiritual
understanding to our conversations, we are gentle with
each other and willing to listen and learn from each
other.

Day after day, year after year, God's presence within
us enhances us individually and enhances our
relationship. How precious is God's love for us and
God's love being expressed by us. Honoring our
relationship with God, we naturally honor our
relationship as a couple.

> "When we cry, 'Abba! Father!' it is
> that very Spirit bearing witness with our spirit
> that we are children of God."
> —Romans 8:15–16

Day 175

We are living in the shelter
of God's love and tender care.

SHELTER OF LOVE Let's never miss a great moment in life because we are expecting the worst to happen at any time. That is living in fear!

So if we sense that an unfounded fear is keeping us from experiencing something meaningful, we pray for courage. Our faith in God will strengthen us and free us to make wise decisions.

Sheltered in God's tender care, we are living in faith, not in fear. We have peace of mind knowing that the spirit of God surrounds us. Wherever we may go and whatever we may do, we are in the shelter of God's love.

God's presence is our blessed assurance. We face all circumstances with faith—our shoulders back and our heads held high—for we are one with God.

**"You will have confidence, because there is hope;
you will be protected and take your rest in safety."
—Job 11:18**

Day 176

—◆—

*The love we give and receive
is from God.*

**GIVING
AND
RECEIVING** In our relationship, we give each
other love and respect. The beauty of
what we are doing is that we are
being blessed by what we do in
blessing each other.

How good it feels to know that our actions help
create an atmosphere of love and harmony in our life
and in the lives of the people who are near and dear to
us. As children of God, we share a sacred kinship. We
love one another for who we are and as we are.

The love we express is more than an emotion—it is a
pure, inner attitude that comes from and is nurtured by
God. Together we rejoice that in and through our
relationship, we give and receive the gift of love to each
other and to everyone in our life.

> "To set the mind on the Spirit
> is life and peace."
> —Romans 8:6

Day 177

*God is our inspiration
in following our dreams.*

**FOLLOW
OUR
DREAMS**

Over time, an unfulfilled dream can be pushed back into the corners of our minds and forgotten. Then, suddenly, in the midst of a conversation or in reflection, it begins to stir in our thoughts and sparks our interest again. Maybe God is telling us that it is time to dust off that dream and make it a reality.

Following the inspiration of God, we begin to implement creative ideas in our life so that our dream does come true. With God guiding us, we are aware of wonderful possibilities and we act on them.

We have opened our life to a new world of possibilities. With this beginning, we have started on a journey that will take us to even greater dreams that await our discovery.

> "Then the Lord came down in a pillar of cloud,
> and stood at the entrance of the tent. . . . And he said,
> 'Hear my words: . . . I the Lord make myself known to
> them in visions; I speak to them in dreams.' "
> —Numbers 12:5–6

DAILY WORD FOR COUPLES

Day 178

— ◆ —

God is our comfort and our strength.

GARDEN OF PRAYER

When our need is to quiet our troubled souls, we turn to God for comfort and peace. As we pray, we visualize a beautiful garden where fragrant flowers of all varieties are blooming. Butterflies are fluttering from one plant to another.

Now let's picture ourselves entering the garden, a sacred place where God waits for us. As we enter, we feel such relief, for we are leaving all worry behind.

In silence, God's love enfolds us, and we are comforted. No words need to be spoken, for God knows what is in our hearts and on our minds. We linger in the garden with God until we feel completely refreshed.

Leaving our garden of prayer, we are at ease and filled with a quiet, unshakable strength that comes from being alone with God, our comfort and our strength.

> "He led them in safety,
> so that they were not afraid."
> —Psalms 78:53

DAILY WORD FOR COUPLES

Day 179

---◆---

Our Prayer

Dear God,

Whenever we are praying about physical health, we pray that our hearts are blessed with strength. These magnificent organs continually circulate nourishment throughout our bodies.

Our hearts are symbolic of our love for each other, and we know that Your love for us will sustain us at all times. If one of us or the both of us are going through a challenge and feel depressed, we pray to be strengthened emotionally. Our life-affirming prayers to You encourage us and are a message of healing for both of us.

Your spirit resides at the heart of our hearts. As we bring all concerns to You, we are relieved of worry. Our prayer times with You are a healing therapy that blesses us and enriches our total well-being.

**"Now that you have purified your souls
by your obedience to the truth so that you
have genuine mutual love, love one another
deeply from the heart."
—1 Peter 1:22**

Day 180

—◆—

My Gift to You

I GIVE YOU THE GIFT OF LOVING MEMORIES.

People may come and go in our life, but we are continuing on in a loving relationship. We are helping each other create a life of purpose and meaning and giving each other loving memories.

I thank God that you are brightening my life. Sharing memories of the things that we have done together and the laughter that we have shared is my gift to you. Together we are creating new memories each day.

God has truly blessed us by giving us the opportunity to love and to be loved by each other. We are both working at not taking our relationship for granted, and I promise to do my best in giving you lasting, loving memories.

With every memory of you, I am envisioning a beautiful and special creation of God's life and love.

> "I do not cease to give thanks for you
> as I remember you in my prayers."
> —Ephesians 1:16

CREATING MEMORIES THAT HEAL

By Peter Rosenberger

Christmas of 1995 was going to be different for my wife, Gracie, and me and our two sons, Parker and Grayson. We were spending this Christmas together at the vacation home of Gracie's parents in Montana. This would be a Christmas like none we had ever experienced as a family. We were there specifically to create healing memories for our family, memories of a Christmas without emergency trips to the hospital, without physical pain for Gracie, and without emotional pain for all four of us.

Gracie and I met in college. We were married in 1986, shortly after her legs had been severely injured in a car wreck. Over the next 10 years, Gracie endured more than 50 surgeries. Most were attempts to save her legs. During this time, she gave birth to Parker and Grayson and she launched a career as a singer. Once she performed a concert while receiving medication through an IV concealed under her clothing.

Even though Gracie went to the hospital every 2 to 3 months for surgery, I was determined that our lives would be as normal as possible. I took Parker and Grayson to visit Gracie often during her hospitalizations. The boys always found a place to lie on Gracie's bed, careful to avoid her IV tubes and casts. They were happy to be close to their mom and learned to be extraordinarily sensitive to people with any kind of difficulty or physical challenge.

Parker and Grayson seemed much more resilient than I was. I felt as if the harder I tried to deal with Gracie's suffering, the less effective I became. In addition, it soon became apparent that I was hung up on my own theology: I believed God was supposed to fix everything and that bad things should not happen to good people like Gracie.

My dad is a minister, and throughout my childhood, I attended Sunday school. As Gracie's suffering continued, I thought, the God who is allowing Gracie to suffer is not the God I learned about in Sunday school! I spent so much time trying to control the situation that I was not capable of experiencing a beautiful, productive relationship with my family or with God. I was angry!

As Gracie struggled for several years to save her right

leg from being amputated and four additional years to save her left leg, I struggled to be in control and to keep my beliefs intact. Ironically enough, Gracie and I both had to let go of our own struggles before we experienced peace.

When Gracie became a double amputee, I took a family medical leave from my job and stayed home for the summer, helping to keep my family intact. I hung up my business suits and ties and put on an apron. I learned to cook, clean, and most important, I learned simply to be with my family.

During that summer, I became aware that although I had been a good caregiver, I had been a lousy husband during the years of our marriage. It took me that long to realize that Gracie's body and Gracie the person are not one and the same and to realize that she needs me to love her as the whole person she truly is. When I quit pushing to force a different life on us and accepted the life we were given, God's peace began to seep into our marriage, our family, and our home.

There are still aspects of our life I don't care for very much. Some days are very difficult, but I find more moments of joy than I ever imagined possible.

Although we have grieved over the loss of her legs, once we began accepting the loss, we started to see the positive benefits of less pain and the physical freedom her Flex-Foot legs gave her. For the first time, she was able to do the everyday "mom stuff" that most of us take for granted. Gracie not only has a fresh outlook on life but she knows that God has given her a new chance to really live life.

Since that first Montana Christmas in 1995, we have made our trip to the Northwest an annual event, building new holiday memories each year. We take four-wheelers into the forest, cut down our own Christmas tree, and bring it back to the house on a sled. We fill our days with skiing, drinking hot cocoa, playing games, and riding snowmobiles into Yellowstone National Park. Waking up each morning, we look out at the snow-covered Rockies and spy deer, elk, and an occasional moose. Watching Gracie ski or take part in any of these things is watching pure joy in action!

I remember one special moment that made my heart overflow: All four of us exited the ski lift and were preparing to go down the slope. Parker took off on his snowboard; Gracie and Grayson shot off down the slope on skis. I hung back for a moment to watch my family: my family—the same family that had huddled around hospital beds year after year—was racing down a snow-covered mountain together. I can't think of a better Christmas memory.

Day 181

—◆—

Thank God for uniting us in love and in life.

HAPPY ANNIVERSARY! Both of us may not acknowledge birthday, engagement, or wedding anniversaries with the same eagerness, yet there is something so gratifying about observing the dates that mark the special events in our life.

When we say, "Happy birthday!" to each other, we are saying, "Thank God that you were born!" When we say, "Happy anniversary!" to each other, we are saying, "Thank God that we are going through life together."

We are kindred spirits that share love and harmony with and within our family. Time can almost seem to stand still and to also rush by. By observing our anniversaries, we are doing more than marking time; we are saying, "Thank God for each other!"

> "How very good and pleasant it is
> when kindred live together in unity!"
> —Psalms 133:1

Day 182

$—\diamond—$

The spirit of God renews us and renews
our enthusiasm for life.

RENEWAL

Once we have completed a project that lasted several days, weeks, or months, we may feel temporarily drained of energy and imagination. Yet when we allow ourselves to think about new projects and goals, we renew our sense of enthusiasm and creativity.

Thanks to God this does happen, because God is our source of renewal. Knowing this, we can recharge ourselves physically and creatively in prayer.

In prayer, the joy of being aware of God fills our souls. Coming away from our prayer time with a fresh outlook, we find that the air seems fresher and the sky even bluer. We are renewed and refreshed!

Our energy is now directed toward new ideas. The spirit of God has renewed us, and we experience a resurgence of our enthusiasm for life!

"Into your hand I commit my spirit;
you have redeemed me, O Lord, faithful God."
—Psalms 31:5

DAILY WORD FOR COUPLES

Day 183

♦

Knowing that God is our help in every need,
we have peace of mind.

COPING

We may not have a choice about what kind of challenges we experience or whether or not we experience challenges. Yet we do have a choice about how we deal with every challenge.

We do not directly control the interest rates on loans, but we do control our interests in life and how we go about pursuing them. Knowing that we do have choices helps us to cope with everyday life.

Yet knowing that God helps us in making choices as we go through a change and as we overcome a challenge gives us peace of mind even in the midst of what may seem like a crisis. With God, we are never left in the dark about any situation in life, about any condition of life. God shines the light of wisdom into the darkness of challenge and reveals what we need to know and to do.

"The light shines in the darkness,
and the darkness did not overcome it."
—John 1:5

Day 184

*God strengthens us from the inside out
and assures us that we are protected.*

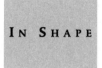

IN SHAPE

Whether we are pulling weeds in the garden or participating in sports, we want to be in physical shape for activities that test our strength, alertness, and agility.

We also want to be in spiritual shape for the usual and unusual activities that await us. Prayer is a powerful way to build ourselves up from the inside out—from the spirit of God within us to the actions we take.

Through prayer, we communicate with God as we talk and listen. We find that we can communicate with our Creator at any time—in urgent matters and in peaceful moments.

Listening to an inner urging or for an unmistakable knowing of what is safe and best for us, we take the high road of cooperating with a divine plan. We are safe and secure in what we do and in the way we do it.

"Protect me, O God, for in you I take refuge."
—Psalms 16:1

Day 185

———◆———

We let go and trust God to guide
and inspire our children.

PARENTING

As parents we knew at the time our children were born that they would eventually go out into the world on their own.

In the meantime, we invested our love, time, and prayers in meeting the sacred responsibility of preparing our children to live happy, successful lives and in preparing ourselves to let our children go.

What we and other parents realize is that although we helped shape our children, God is the one who created them. And they have been created to thrive.

God is the guiding light that illumines their way. We can and do let go of doubt or fear about these precious children and know that God will provide the wisdom and inspiration they need. We trust God completely.

"Trust in the Lord forever,
for in the Lord God
you have an everlasting rock."
—Isaiah 26:4

Day 186

———◆———

When we lean on each other for support,
we are beholding the presence of God in each other.

LEANING ON EACH OTHER

When we feel as if we need to lean on each other for strength or confidence, we are simply going outside ourselves for what is always within us. Yet during those times of supporting each other, we strengthen our bond with our commitment to being a loving couple.

At times we may be more aware of each other's strengths than we are of our own. We know that at such times we are beholding the presence of God in each other. Then as we reflect the holy presence back to each other, we are reminded to look within. As we do, we become two pillars of strength that support a fulfilling, long-lasting relationship.

Leaning on each other, we are leaning on the presence of God in each other.

> "For they call themselves after the holy city,
> and lean on the God of Israel;
> the Lord of hosts is his name."
> —Isaiah 48:2

Day 187

—◆—

Through our positive attitudes, we are tuning ourselves to the wonder of God.

POSITIVE ATTITUDE There is so much we appreciate about each other, and one thing that we never grow tired of telling each other we appreciate is our positive attitude. We have a way of seeing the bright side of every situation and helping each other understand that there is some good that will come from every situation.

Yet when we start praising each other, we admit that it is God's spirit within us that gives hope and understanding. We might go on to say that it is God's spirit within us that identifies the truth of hope that we speak about.

We are thankful to know how much we each value the other's positive attitude. As we open our hearts and minds to the blessings that God has prepared for us, we understand that God is revealing the wonder of life in us and through us.

> "For you, O Lord, are my hope,
> my trust, O Lord, from my youth."
> —Psalms 71:5

Day 188

*Our family is a sacred circle
of God's creations.*

EXPANDING OUR CIRCLE Whether we are expanding our family circle with the inclusion of children or pets, family or friends, we are inviting the love of God to move from within us out to others.

Marriage and birth, adoption and friendship will continually add to our sacred circle. Death and separation may seem to make our physical circle smaller, but our spiritual bond with loved ones can never be broken. Our circle of life and love is continually expanding to include more and to be more.

Every person, every pet is important to us and revered by us. We feel the pleasure that comes as we honor God's creations and accept them into our life and our family. There is always room for more in our circle because we always have more love to give.

> **"And the King will answer them, 'Truly I tell you,
> just as you did it to one of the least of these
> who are members of my family, you did it to me.'"**
> **—Matthew 25:40**

Day 189

---◆---

*A few moments in silence with God
refresh and renew us.*

**GOD
MOMENTS**
We may not realize how much we
have needed to get away from our
routine for a few days or a few weeks
until we are on vacation. Here, a
cheerful birdsong or gently falling rain awakens us so
much more gently than the sound of an alarm clock.

What do we do when we are stressed by the hurried
atmosphere in which we live and work? We may not be
able to retreat to a tranquil place, but we can answer the
call that Jesus gave to His disciples: "Come away to a
deserted place all by yourselves and rest a while." (Mark
6:31) Our journey is an inner one that takes us to the
sacred atmosphere of our souls. A few moments in
silence, focused on the presence of God, refresh us.

We return from our communion with the Creator
appreciating how time alone with God renews us.

"You were taught to put away your former way of life . . .
and to be renewed in the spirit of your minds, and to
clothe yourselves with the new self, created according
to the likeness of God in true righteousness and holiness."
—Ephesians 4:22–24

Day 190

—◆—

With our love for and respect of each other, we are fully developing and enjoying our relationship.

MATURING TOGETHER A few wrinkles and a gray hair or two are not the only or even the first signs of maturity. The respect and caring we have for each other and our marriage are declarations that we are maturing together. We are devoting time and prayer to fully developing our relationship and enjoying the results of a maturity that enriches us both.

Each day, we are learning and growing, and we are building on the love and accomplishments of all our yesterdays. Enjoying the present time, we look forward to even greater times. Because we are maturing, our relationship is maturing also.

We will forever sense a sweet mystery about each other, but we also have a history of our love for and confidence in each other.

"They are to do good, to be rich in good works, generous, and ready to share, thus storing up for themselves the treasure of a good foundation for the future, so that they may take hold of the life that really is life."
—1 Timothy 6:18

Day 191

—◆—

*Our mutual admiration adds so much meaning
and pleasure to our life.*

**ADMIRING
EACH
OTHER**
Because we hold each other in such
high regard, we experience pleasure in
giving each other attention and
consideration. With mutual admiration,
we make our life together one of exceptional love and
understanding.

We let the love of God express wonderful words and
actions through us in our everyday life. We are willing
to be loved. With that willingness, we allow each other
to know our deepest thoughts and feelings, and we
especially admire the courage it takes to do just that.

We have found each other and also discovered how
meaningful life can be when the two of us are dedicated
to finding something new to admire about each other
every day.

"The kingdom of heaven is like treasure hidden
in a field, which someone found and hid;
then in his joy he goes and sells all that he has
and buys that field."
—Matthew 13:44

Day 192

Through our commitment to God,
we bless ourselves and we bless others.

COMMITMENT TO GOD

With our commitment to God, we are inviting divine love to be expressed in our thoughts and in our actions.

At every moment, we listen for God's guidance and instruction. Divinely guided, we care about and for each other. We go willingly to bring a caring touch to friends and family who need our help and encouragement.

We consecrate our hands as instruments of comfort and our words as declarations of peace. God is the inspiration for every kind word we speak and the tenderness in every touch we give.

With our commitment to serving God, we are dedicated to being a blessing to each other and to others.

"I told them that the hand of my God had been gracious
upon me, and also the words that the king had spoken
to me. Then they said, 'Let us start building!'
So they committed themselves to the common good."
—Nehemiah 2:18

DAILY WORD FOR COUPLES

Day 193

---◆---

We place our faith and trust in God's wisdom,
and we are fulfilled.

FULFILLED We are fulfilled in every way. Our fulfillment comes from the blessings that God has given us. God has blessed us with healthy minds and bodies, with renewal and healing.

We are one in spirit with God in every moment. Before we speak the words of our prayers, God hears us and has an answer for us. Every need is being met according to the love of God.

We have an abundance of love—from God, from each other, from friends and family—to sustain us throughout eternity. Love empowers us to do the best that we can in everything that we do.

We are fulfilled in every way, for God is all that we will ever need.

> **"God will fully satisfy every need**
> **of yours according to his riches."**
> **—Philippians 4:19**

Day 194

---◆---

Our Prayer

Dear God,

Why is it that sometimes when we want and need so badly to sleep, we have a difficult time going to sleep? To avoid feeling anxious during that quiet, still time of waiting to fall asleep, we pray. We pray ourselves to sleep.

God, as we acknowledge Your presence within and around us, we relax. The more we fill our minds with thoughts of You, the more peace of mind we experience.

By tomorrow, today's challenges and situations will be history. We have learned from them, but what we have learned more than anything else is that You are our peace and serenity.

We gently let go of every concern and drift off into a time of complete rest and renewal. Supported by Your loving presence, God, we can and do find peaceful, restful sleep.

"I will both lie down and sleep in peace;
for you alone, O Lord, make me lie down in safety."
—Psalms 4:8

Day 195

———◆———

My Gift to You

I GIVE YOU THE GIFT OF MY UNDIVIDED ATTENTION.

Giving you my undivided attention does not mean that I must have an answer when you are questioning what to do about a problem with a coworker or a project. I may be of most help to you by simply listening.

Then there may be other times that I say or do something that will reveal a workable solution to a dilemma.

When I am focusing on you, when I am truly listening to you, I will know when to offer a suggestion and when to give you a hug. When I give you a sincere compliment on how well you look, I am letting you know that you have my attention, and I like what I see.

There is something quite magnetic in one of us giving the other attention; it encourages us both to be attentive to and caring of each other.

> "Pay attention to what you hear; the measure
> you give will be the measure you get,
> and still more will be given you."
> —Mark 4:24

Day 196

♦

*From this time on, we remain aware of God
and aware of each other.*

FROM THIS TIME ON Every day God gives us a blank page on which to create a fresh start. If a disagreement marred the previous day, we start the next day fresh, allowing forgiveness to wipe the page clean so that we can begin again.

From this time on, we take whatever time is necessary to clear any past misunderstandings and allow the peace of God to fill our relationship with love and forgiveness.

From this time on, we make a conscious effort to be constantly aware of each other's concerns and feelings.

From this time on, we dedicate ourselves to filling each day with love and understanding and to ending it on a positive note.

From this time on, we remember that in every situation, God will show us a way. We rejoice in the blessings we share, and we look forward to the ones that tomorrow will bring.

"At this moment he is praying."
—Acts 9:11

Day 197

— ◆ —

*Our perception is a view of our world
that is inspired by God.*

PERCEPTION

How we react to any situation is closely tied to our perception of what is taking place. Because we want our perception to go beyond the appearances of that moment, we rely on spiritual insight. Then we are able to respond from the understanding of knowing what to do and say. Prayer is an effective way to gain a perspective inspired by our Creator.

We thank God for the spiritual insight to see the truth within every situation. God helps us understand what is most important concerning any decisions we may need to make.

God encourages us not to let emotions interfere with good judgment. With God guiding our thoughts, we are focused on the blessing that is within each situation. We are grateful for a perspective that views all with spiritual understanding.

"Those who believe in me, even though
they die, will live, and everyone who lives and believes
in me will never die. Do you believe this?"
—John 11:25, 26

Day 198

—◆—

*Our souls awaken to the joy
and beauty of God each day.*

WAKE UP! Familiar sights may take on bright, new appeal for us as we watch each other seeing them for the first time or after a long time. The excitement we share is a wake-up call that heightens our awareness of our surroundings.

We never want to take the majesty of God's world for granted. So we give ourselves a wake-up call to life when we take time to experience the beauty and diversity of our world.

With our senses awakened, we encourage each other to enjoy the wonders of our world—from the seemingly insignificant to the most apparent. With every sight, touch, taste, smell, and sound, we are aware of the glory of God's creative mastery. Our souls continue to awaken to the joy and beauty of God.

"I will give thanks to the Lord with my whole heart;
I will tell of all your wonderful deeds."
—Psalms 9:1

Day 199

---◆---

Living in an awareness of God's presence,
we are always at home.

HOME
A well-known adage declares that home is where the heart is. Because our hearts are filled with the love of God, we are at home wherever we are.

If we are selling our house, we pray for divine guidance in finding the right real estate agent and the perfect buyer.

In searching for a new home, we pray for divine guidance in finding the right one. More than just structure, our new home will be a haven where we will dwell in the comfort and peace of God.

Before we move to a new house or apartment, we acknowledge that God has been with us wherever we have lived and will be with us wherever we will live. We know that we are always at home with God.

> **"O Lord, I love the house in which you dwell,**
> **and the place where your glory abides."**
> **—Psalms 26:8**

Day 200

—◆—

God serves as our example
in setting our family values.

FAMILY VALUES

We would be hard pressed to recall every person who has made an important difference in our lives, but we have no difficulty recognizing the values our parents and other family members taught us during our growing-up years. Knowing this, we are aware of how important it is for us to set a good example through our family values.

In all matters and at all times, we are patient and understanding. We have the ultimate parent, God, who shows us the power of good that is expressed in unconditional love, and we follow God's guidance in loving our family.

We live as examples of how honesty and integrity serve to strengthen a relationship. Peace is an integral part of our value system. The family values we live by today are being passed along to our children so that the value of love, patience, and understanding will be shared in the families of future generations.

> "The earth will be filled with the knowledge
> of the glory of the Lord."—Habakkuk 2:14

Day 201

We are vitally alive!

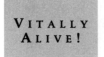

When our hands touch, we feel the joy that being together brings us. From that tender touch, we share a moment of peace with each other, and we experience a gladness that comes from being alive and being alert to the presence of God within.

What a tremendous sense of joy and reassurance we feel as we hold hands. We feel the warmth of life emanating from each other, flowing from one to the other. What a treasure our time of closeness is.

All that we do together, we do in love and joy. Whether we are doing chores around our home, enjoying a time of relaxation, or working at our jobs, we do so with an appreciation of being vitally alive.

God's unlimited love enhances our love for each other. Our words, our thoughts, and our actions all reflect the sense of wonder we experience in being alive to the presence of God.

"This is eternal life."
—John 17:3

DAILY WORD FOR COUPLES

Day 202

— ◆ —

*Through the years, we have accomplished much
by working with God and with each other.*

**THROUGH
THE
YEARS** We have made it through times that
called on us to be more than we had
ever imagined we could be. We have
shown courage that helped each other
when we felt helpless ourselves. We have been tender
with each other when we felt so overwhelmed that the
only way we knew to express our love was through
gentle words and quiet actions.

Through it all, we may have had moments of doubt,
but God kept telling us that we could make it together.
As we worked with God and with each other, we did
make it—through even the toughest of challenges.

Through the years, we may have missed out in
reaching some of our goals, but we have accomplished
far more than we ever dreamed we could. And we did it
together.

> **"We know that all things work together
> for good for those who love God, who are called
> according to his purpose."**
> **—Romans 8:28**

Day 203

*A newborn is a gift from God, coming
into the world to bless and be blessed.*

**BLESSING
A NEW
LIFE**

Holding our newborn baby in our
arms, we feel a surge of thanksgiving
for life. As we gaze into the face of pure
innocence, we realize what a creation
of God's love, what an extension of our love this
precious one is. Whispering words of encouragement,
we know that in reality we are offering a prayer in honor
of our child:

"Welcome to the world, little one. Your life is a gift
that has already blessed us and has already touched the
lives of others, for many are giving thanks for your
arrival.

"We pray that your life will be filled with joy, your
days will be filled with laughter, and your nights will be
filled with peace. Remember to store within your soul
every experience of discovering the miracles of God's
world. Know that God is with you wherever you go
and that you are always in our prayers."

**"Let the little children come to me, and do not stop them;
for it is to such as these that the kingdom
of heaven belongs."—Matthew 19:14**

DAILY WORD FOR COUPLES

Day 204

—◆—

*We see the glory of God reflected by us
and all around us.*

**E N J O Y
T H E
J O U R N E Y**

As we travel on vacation, we enjoy seeing unfamiliar scenery and exploring new areas of interest.

Likewise, when friends or loved ones visit us, they, too, view our familiar sights with a sense of newness and wonder. Seeing the look of enjoyment on the faces of our visitors reminds us to appreciate the beauty and uniqueness of our surroundings. Then we take another look, seeing past the familiar to the miracle-working power of God that has gone into the creation of each plant, animal, and person.

No matter how busy our responsibilities at home and on the job may keep us, we can find a few moments to pause and behold the glory of God reflected in our surroundings.

Looking at the familiar with a fresh appreciation, we take time to enjoy every day of our journey in life.

**"I know that there is nothing better
for them than to be happy and enjoy themselves
as long as they live."
—Ecclesiastes 3:12**

Day 205

———◆———

Knowing that God is our constant guide,
we have a positive outlook in all situations.

POSITIVE OUTLOOK

Looking at a glass of water, do we see it as half full or half empty? We may not always agree on every matter, but we can agree to look at everything with a positive outlook. Then as we take a close look—whether it is regarding a person, place, or situation—we acknowledge that good is present.

For instance, because of rain, our plan of being outdoors may change into doing something indoors. We thank God that we are able to make a choice and may go on to enjoy a visit to the museum.

If someone we care about does or says something we may not agree with, we acknowledge that God, not us, is in charge of this person's life. We thank God for guiding our loved one on right paths.

Keeping a positive outlook keeps us enthusiastic about life and keeps us alert to the good that will appear no matter what turn our life may take.

"I can do all things through him
who strengthens me."
—Philippians 4:13

Day 206

❖

*We treasure the cherished moments
we spend together.*

CHERISHED MOMENTS We have not recorded every significant event in our life on film or in photographs. Yet we have memories that capture cherished moments and how we felt as we experienced them. How good it is now to reminisce about these precious times and to relive the joy that we shared in the past.

We are given more and more of these cherished moments because God is continually blessing us with wonder to experience and to enjoy. God is with us in every moment of life, so every moment is sacred.

Recognizing our life as the divine blessing that it is, we welcome cherished moments of expressing our faith and enjoying each other. As we store sacred moments in our memories, we feel a blessed re-awakening to the assurance that we now are and always will be blessed by God.

**"I am with you, says the Lord."
—Haggai 1:13**

Day 207
—◆—

*We celebrate life by giving thanks for life
and for our partnership in life.*

CELEBRATING LIFE

Let's celebrate life! One of the highest forms of celebration that we can participate in is our heartfelt thanksgiving to God. Our thanksgiving may sound something like this: "God, we are thankful for life, which encompasses health of mind and body. We are so thankful that we have blended our individual lives to create a devoted partnership that enriches and strengthens us both."

We may decide our celebration includes a walk on our favorite nature trail or a visit with family and friends. Spending time together doing nothing else but enjoying each other's company would be a quiet but truly meaningful celebration.

No matter how we choose to celebrate life, we acknowledge God as the giver and sustainer of life. This is an inner celebration that is conveyed in all that we do.

"They shall celebrate the fame
of your abundant goodness, and shall
sing aloud of your righteousness."
—Psalms 145:7

DAILY WORD FOR COUPLES

Day 208

God's presence guides us on our way.

SMOOTH SAILING The calm surface of a lake can quickly erupt into choppy waves as the wind of an approaching storm hits. If we are sailing on the lake, we will more than likely be challenged by the storm as we try to reach the shore.

As we share life together, we have no guarantee that we will always experience smooth sailing, but we do have the assurance that in good times and challenging times God will be there with us, guiding us along the way.

Our faith keeps us strong and gives us the courage we need to continue on. Even when the going is rough, God's presence will be the wind in our sails that moves us in the right direction. We overcome each challenge, for God leaves no area of our life to chance.

> "I saw the Lord always before me,
> for he is at my right hand so that I
> will not be shaken."
> —Acts 2:25

DAILY WORD FOR COUPLES

Day 209

---◆---

Our Prayer

Dear God,

Our love for You and for each other fills us with joy. We let that joy flow out from us so that it is included in everything we say and do.

When we look at each other as the person who has made a commitment to share a life, we see each other through the eyes of love.

With eyes of love, we see that we are doing everything possible to keep our relationship strong and joy-filled. Our expressions of love are freely given. When we embrace, we know how love and reassurance feel.

Your love reaches out from us to each other, and every day, we are learning how to express more of Your love to each other. We are grateful to You, God. Thank You for love and for loving us. Thank You for allowing us to see each other through the eyes of love.

> "Let your light shine before others, so that they may see your good works and give glory to your Father in heaven."
> —Matthew 5:16

Day 210

—◆—

My Gift to You

I GIVE YOU THE GIFT OF MY SUPPORT.

I gladly give you support toward accomplishing your heart's desires. Some decisions you make may have a greater impact on our life than others, but I want you to know that I will support you from the beginning till the completion of your endeavors.

If you are pursuing a career move or furthering your education, I will help you in every way that I can—with my prayers, with my words of encouragement, with my willingness to help out in whatever way possible.

I love you, and the gift of my support is one way I can express my love so that it helps you achieve what is meaningful and important to you and to our family.

My support of you is a natural expression of my confidence in God to bring about great things through you and me.

> "Surely then you will lift up your face . . .
> you will be secure, and will not fear."
> —Job 11:15

A CHANGE OF HEART

BY GRACIE ROSENBERGER

When I was 17 years old, I fell asleep while driving and crashed my car. For the next 3 weeks, I was unconscious and in critical condition. When I awoke from the coma, I managed to mumble a question even though my jaws had been wired shut. "Did I hurt anybody?" I asked. "No one was hurt but you," was the grim answer. "You were alone in the car when you fell asleep and hit a cement abutment—head-on."

I had internal injuries, and almost every bone from my waist down was crushed. I lay flat on my back in traction for weeks. During that time, I had a lot of time to think about my life and my faith. I questioned if either was still intact and if I believed what I learned about God in childhood.

My faith began when Holocaust survivor Corrie ten Boom told me about God's love. She and her family rescued many Jews during the Nazi occupation of Holland. Eventually Corrie and her family were imprisoned in a concentration camp. Corrie survived and wrote their story in a book, *The Hiding Place*. This amazing woman not only survived the pain and hardships of the camp; she came out of it all with an even stronger faith.

Over the years, my faith grew, but lying in that hospital bed, I secretly wondered if my body or faith could survive this terrible ordeal. However small my faith, I slowly improved. In fact, 2 years and a couple of dozen surgeries later, I returned to college where I met Peter, and we married in August of 1986.

Yet, I lived in denial about the severity of my injuries and the excruciating pain I dealt with constantly. This denial allowed me to live in a fantasy world where I believed marriage would somehow fix my body and take away my pain. When the marriage didn't fix anything, I was sure that having children and my first record deal as a singer would somehow make right all the things that were wrong and too painful for me.

In the next few years, I did have two beautiful children, Parker and Grayson, and my singing career did take off. Yet, the deterioration of my legs continued. As the number of surgeries increased, Peter slipped more and more into the role of my caregiver, but his role as my husband was pushed more and more into the background.

There seemed to be no love in our home, and I searched throughout the Bible for some justification that would release me from my marriage.

Praying for a miracle time and time again, I wanted to wake up one morning with perfect legs, with no more scars and no more pain. It didn't happen, and even after 50 surgeries, I didn't get better. In order to walk, I used crutches or a cedar cane my dad had made for me. Our house was not equipped for a wheelchair, so when I had blisters from using crutches or when the pain just got to be too unbearable for me to walk, I crawled!

When Peter saw me crawling from room to room, he became even more angry. I related my physical pain to the emotional pain of our marriage. I thought, If I get out of this marriage, my physical pain will ease. I became more depressed, and Peter became angrier.

Finally, after years of struggling, Peter and I gave up. I prayed, "Lord, if you want me to stay married to this man, You have to give me a change of heart concerning everything about him and our marriage." I had no idea the Peter was praying for a change of heart also in order to stay with me.

The change of heart did come—for both of us. God chipped away at the wall I had built to protect myself from Peter's anger. God led Peter in rediscovering my good points, the very attributes that had caused him to fall in love with me when we first met. We stopped blaming God and blaming each other. We began to understand that God had already given us hearts full of love for each other. We knew that what was needed was for us to be willing to give and receive that love as a gift.

All of this did not happen overnight, but it did happen. Slowly, over time, the anger and depression lifted. Now, I can honestly say, the real miracle my soul needed was not the physical kind, but of the heart.

Part of the result of that change of heart was my decision to lose my legs. I had battled for so long to save them, but when I gave them up, my life greatly improved.

I have wonderful state-of-the-art Flex-Foot prosthetic legs that enable me to do more than I ever dared dream of doing with my damaged legs. I snow ski, jump on the trampoline with my boys, and maintain a national speaking and singing schedule. I am learning to rock climb!

I still have to put my legs on every morning and take them off every night, but when I do, I am reminded of how grateful I am to lead an active life that is filled with love. I certainly don't want to go through all I have gone through again, but I am exceedingly thankful for what I learned about faith and life, for what I have discovered in my marriage and family life. All this happened because Peter and I asked God for a change of hearts.

Day 211

◆

*God is the source of serenity
within our souls.*

INNER PEACE

From the youngest child to the most mature adult, everyone longs to experience the blessed tranquillity of inner peace, and we are no exception. This serenity of the soul comes to us as we open ourselves to an awareness of God within us and within every moment of our life. With our total commitment, we acknowledge that being aware of God is our reason for being. How blessed we feel in keeping that sacred commitment.

In prayer, God gently reminds us: "Dear ones, there is no way that you could ever be separated from Me nor will there ever be a time that you are without My love. It is My spirit that enlivens you. You are now and will be forevermore in My presence. Now be at peace. Be at peace."

**"I pray that, according to the riches of his glory,
he may grant that you may be strengthened
in your inner being with power through his Spirit."
—Ephesians 3:16**

Day 212

—◆—

Oh, how simply glorious God's world is!

SIMPLICITY Drawing on the wisdom of God's spirit within us, we make life simpler. In order for our life to be less complicated, we know not to let anyone or anything interfere with our awareness of God and the glory of God.

Making our life less complicated may be easier said than done, but achieving anything worthwhile requires time and attention. Most often it is the simple things, the things we have taken for granted, that mean so much to us.

Do we remember when we last experienced a sunrise? Waking early to watch the brilliant sun coming from beyond the horizon, we are treated to awesome beauty. As the stillness of the night gives way to songbirds, we hear a message to live life fully.

How simply glorious God's world is!

> "The heavens are telling the glory of God;
> and the firmament proclaims his handiwork."
> —Psalms 19:1

DAILY WORD FOR COUPLES

Day 213

*Life is a melody that resounds throughout
our world and within our souls.*

**MELODY
OF LIFE**

The laughter of children at play, the
rustling of leaves in the wind, the
rippling of water in a stream—all
contribute to a beautiful melody of
life. This melody is one that has resounded throughout
time and will continue on throughout eternity. Life has
a melody all its own, and it plays a tune of joy within
our souls.

We, too, are part of this melody of life, adding our
own unique notes to blend with the notes of all
creation. Our loving words blend together in a harmony
that resonates with the melody of life around us.

What joy we feel in knowing that we are important
to the melody of life, for we are two of God's
magnificent creations.

> **"Our mouth was filled with laughter,
> and our tongue with shouts of joy."
> —Psalms 126:2**

Day 214

---◆---

*Keeping our focus on the presence of God
within brings clarity to our life.*

FOCUS

Looking at a moving wheel, we can
see the whir of motion along the outer
rim. Yet the hub at the center appears
to remain perfectly still. That hub,
which stays in focus for us physically, reminds us to
remain focused spiritually—on the presence of God at
the core of our beings.

Despite the turbulence around us, we can remain
focused and centered on the presence of God within us.
With our attention on God and by keeping it there, we
will find the answers to any questions we may have
and the solutions to any problems that we may face.

God's presence within us is unchanging and constant.
In God's presence, we receive love and acceptance that
enable us to view the world with greater understanding.

> "How much better to get wisdom than gold!
> To get understanding is
> to be chosen rather than silver."
> —Proverbs 16:16

Day 215

---◆---

We are courageous because the grace of God strengthens and reassures us.

COURAGE

We have courage in the face of difficulty because we have a strength of spirit that is expressed as physical, emotional, and mental capabilities. We are courageous because we know that through the grace of God, we can be strong, wise, and effective in whatever is ours to do.

Whenever we have to be apart, we experience grace as God's love filling any emptiness in our hearts and any lonely times in our days and nights with a sacred assurance. Grace helps us to know that we share a spiritual bond with each other that can never be broken. We are courageous!

The grace of God is the love of God soothing us as we are going through a challenge. From this sacred love, we can and do draw on unlimited strength and understanding. We are courageous!

> "Let us therefore approach the throne of grace with boldness, so that we may receive mercy and find grace to help in time of need."
> —Hebrews 4:16

Day 216

—◆—

Our consideration of each other is a way
of being blessed by the very blessing we give.

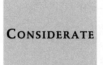

CONSIDERATE We are considerate; we respect each other's thoughts and feelings. This consideration helps us to avoid having regrets about our conversations with and treatment of each other.

There is a kindness and gentleness that moves through our conversations and even through our silence that gives both of us tremendous support. We strengthen each other's resolve to be honest and positive, wise and compassionate.

Our consideration of each other is generated by our commitment to respond from the spirit of God within us rather than react from feelings. And we realize so much pleasure from what we are doing for each other that we feel great ourselves. The consideration we give returns to bless us.

"Those who are kind reward themselves."
—Proverbs 11:17

Day 217

We keep on keeping on together.

KEEP ON KEEPING ON

Why does it seem that the nearer we get to reaching a goal, the harder the going gets? Our bodies tenaciously hold on to those last few pounds we are trying to lose. The supplies we bought for redecorating the living room are off: We may have buckets of paint left over but have run short of wallpaper that is now out of stock.

How do we keep on keeping on in the face of disappointment and problems? One of the best things we can do is pray about the situation. We do not ask God to fix it; we ask God to show us how we can make it better.

Maybe all that we need to do is to give the situation a bit more of our time and patience. With frustration out of the way, we think clearly and we act decisively. We keep on keeping on.

> "Keep on doing the things that you
> have learned and received and heard and seen in me,
> and the God of peace will be with you."
> —Philippians 4:9

Day 218

———◆———

*The love, life, and wisdom of God living out
through us blesses us.*

BLESSED God satisfies the longing of our souls and enriches all of our experiences. Knowing that God is our creator, our companion, our protector, and so much more is a message of hope and healing that reaches down to the depths of our souls and blesses us.

We are prosperous because we know God. We know that God's spirit is within us, and we know that God's presence goes with us wherever we go.

On the darkest night, God lights our way. During the most confusing times, God is our serenity. We cannot buy or trade or earn what God is offering us freely and completely in every moment: the love, life, and wisdom of our Creator.

"God, thank You for enriching our life, for You alone are our prosperity!"

> "My soul is satisfied as with a rich feast,
> and my mouth praises you with joyful lips."
> —Psalms 63:5

Day 219

---◆---

*We are healthy and whole creations
of the Master Builder.*

**HEALTHY
AND
WHOLE**

All life in the universe—from the smallest to the most immense—is made up of tiny particles called atoms. Within those atoms, the Master Builder has included a plan of ongoing life and healing.

We are creations of the Master Builder, created to be healthy and whole and to remain healthy and whole. Within each of our body's genetic blueprint, a plan for a vitally alive and healthy person is imprinted.

We have faith in God and God's healing life within us. Our faith is the foundation of daily living on which we are building a full and active life. We are healthy and whole creations of the Master Builder.

"That one is like a man building a house,
who dug deeply and laid the foundation on rock;
when a flood arose, the river burst against
that house but could not shake it, because it
had been well built."
—Luke 6:48

Day 220

*Drawing from the peace of God within our souls,
we live in harmony with each other.*

**LIVING
IN
HARMONY**
We take a moment now to experience the peace of God with our whole beings. Calm and relaxed, we let our thoughts of God inspire us to be at peace.

In the quiet with God, we connect with the power that dissipates any feelings that would keep us from being a positive, loving couple. How good we feel being in harmony with the spirit of God within us.

Now we bring that experience of harmony back with us to our relationship and the activities of our day. It is amazing how, drawing from the peace of God, we don't let minor or major challenges disturb the calm peace of our souls.

We live in harmony with each other as we live from the peace of God within our souls.

"Finally, brothers and sisters, farewell. Put things in order, listen to my appeal, agree with one another, live in peace; and the God of love and peace will be with you."
—2 Corinthians 13:11

Day 221

— ◆ —

*God is the wisdom that guides us
and the light that inspires us.*

**DIVINE
WISDOM**

We know that God is always with us, guiding us through the most difficult times. God guides us in making the decisions that affect our own well-being and the well-being of our family and friends.

God is the wisdom that is resounding within our souls. With that divine wisdom, God is giving us spiritual understanding that we can rely on no matter how complicated a situation may seem.

We rest in the presence of God and bask in the light of life that is filling us and enfolding us in its healing glow.

As we continue to seek the higher road in life, we know that wherever our footsteps take us, God is there. Everywhere we go, God goes with us.

> **"They turn round and round by his guidance,
> to accomplish all that he commands them
> on the face of the habitable world."**
> **—Job 37:12**

Day 222

*We are explorers of Spirit in
a glorious adventure called life.*

EXPLORERS

God has blessed us with life and
continues to bless us with opportunities
to discover more about ourselves and
the magnificent world in which we live.
In this grand adventure called life, we are explorers
who are eager to learn more about our own spirituality
and the presence and power of God in all and
through all.

Our quest takes us forward to a greater
understanding of our purpose in life and to a greater
awareness of all the blessings God has given us.

As explorers of Spirit, we are ready to discover God
everywhere and we do. Knowing that we are spiritual
beings, we live the abundant life that God created us
to live.

"They said to them, 'Go, explore the land.'
When they came to the hill country of Ephraim . . .
they said to him, 'Inquire of God that we may know
whether the mission we are undertaking will succeed.'
The priest replied, 'Go in peace. The mission you are on
is under the eye of the Lord.' "—Judges 18:2, 5–6

DAILY WORD FOR COUPLES

Day 223

——◆——

We care for each other in considerate,
loving ways.

SPECIAL CARE

We *want* only the best for each other—so in everything we do, we take special care to *do* our best for each other.

The time and attention we give to each other strengthens and enhances our relationship. We understand that the very spirit of God unites us and encourages us to be caring and loving toward each other.

If we have different views on a matter, we each take special care to honor the feelings and opinions of the other.

God is our source of peace, and God guides us gently and lovingly to the right words to say and the caring actions to take.

Moment by moment, day by day, the consideration and loving care we give to each other add up to a lifetime of joy and happiness.

> "Listen, children, to a father's instruction,
> and be attentive, that you may gain insight."
> —Proverbs 4:1

Day 224

Our Prayer

Dear God,

In a prayerful attitude, we become still, close our eyes, and take a few deep breaths. We continue in prayer by breathing evenly and listening with our entire beings. Our prayers are the silent questions within our hearts that only You know and that only You can answer.

We don't listen for audible words. The answer from You may come in that time of prayer as a certain knowing within our souls, or it may come later as a gentle nudge to do or say something. We cannot explain how we know, but we know when You have spoken to us.

Our spiritual journey is uniquely our own, and the guidance we receive from You may come in many different ways. Listening in the quiet of prayer, we prepare ourselves to receive Your answer—in that time of silence or even later during some busy activity.

We listen, God, as You speak to us.

"Call to me and I will answer you."—Jeremiah 33:3

Day 225

—◆—

My Gift to You

**I GIVE YOU THE GIFT
OF COMFORT.**

I wish I could always fix situations for you so that
you never have to be sad or disappointed. Although I
cannot do this, I can be your compassionate friend
and supporter as I hold you in prayer and hold you in
my arms.

I know you so well that I pick up on what you may be
thinking and feeling. So I watch and respond when you
need a word of love or encouragement. Still I may not be
aware that you are going through a challenging time, so
let me know when and how I can be of help to you.

You have comforted me so many times, and I want
to do the same for you. Sometimes we both have
experienced physical and emotional pain that was
beyond each other's ability to be of help. Then we
turned to God, our comfort in every need and every
hour. We are a comfort to each other, and God is the
source of all the comfort we express.

> "The Lord has comforted his people, and will
> have compassion on his suffering ones."
> —Isaiah 49:13

Day 226

*As we forgive, we release burdens
from the past.*

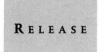

RELEASE

People can be so caught up in negative events from the past that they carry the burden of them for years. When something or someone reminds them of that event, they experience a resurgence of negative feelings.

There is a solution to such a dilemma: Burdens can be cast off through an act of forgiveness. So whenever we need to free ourselves from a burden of the past, we forgive everyone involved—ourselves and others and even those who are no longer part of our life.

Others may not be aware that we are thinking of them, but we know that our prayers will be welcomed by God and that forgiveness blesses our hearts and minds.

As we forgive, we break the bonds of negativity, and our souls leap with the joy of being unburdened.

> **"Love one another with mutual affection;
> outdo one another in showing honor."**
> **—Romans 12:10**

Day 227

—◆—

*We invest our time in whatever enriches our life
with meaning and purpose.*

INVESTING OUR TIME Does it seem that all we need to do today will never fit into the time of one day? Prioritizing how and with whom we spend our time can seem like an impossible task, yet when we decide what is truly important to us and to the ones we love, we put first things first.

And what is most important in doing this is having peace of mind about what we are doing. We find that peace of mind and maintain it through our daily prayer times.

We feel such peace when we are totally in God's presence. With God, we have true peace of mind that enables us to view complex situations with new insight. We make decisions and feel at peace about them.

Instead of wasting time in worrying, we invest our time in what enriches our life with meaning and purpose.

"But do not ignore this one fact, beloved, that
with the Lord one day is like a thousand years, and
a thousand years are like one day."—2 Peter 3:8

Day 228

*God is our sure and present help at any time
of the day or night.*

**EVER-
PRESENT
HELP**

As children, we were blessed to have parents, teachers, and other adults to call upon for help in understanding our world and what we could give and receive in life.

Still today we have all the help we could ever need, for God is our ever-present help. Through all of our experiences, we can call upon God. At any time of need—day or night—God is our sure and present help.

Our sense of security remains with us at all times for the peace, poise, and power of God are with us at all times. We know the security of being enfolded in God's loving embrace. Physically, emotionally, and spiritually we are centered in and focused on God's presence.

> **"Let your steadfast love and
> your faithfulness keep me safe forever."**
> **—Psalms 40:11**

Day 229

The wonder of God uplifts us.

UP MOMENTS Our hearts and souls are uplifted by God's presence. Aware of God's spirit within us and all around us, we are awakened to the wholeness and holiness of life. We understand that we are whole and holy beings.

We feel the joy of being immersed in an awareness of God and the creativity of God. With this awareness, we experience so much more of life every day. We experience such awe in knowing that we are God's creations.

Nothing can get us down because God is our constant, unfailing source of life, love, and understanding. Beyond the wonder that we are aware of through our physical senses, there is the wonder of God within that our spiritual awareness reveals to us.

Oh, what glory God is!

> "Lift up your heads, O gates!
> and be lifted up, O ancient doors!
> that the King of glory may come in."
> —Psalms 24:7

Day 230

—◆—

*During a prayer break, God restores
the peace of our souls.*

**THE
GREAT
ESCAPE**
Our activities at home or at work,
along with other responsibilities,
certainly keep us busy. Yet we feel
great joy in knowing that our activities
are God-directed and bring meaning to our life.

If things become too hectic, we understand that we
can take a prayer break—to get away from the hustle
and bustle of life so that we can be renewed.

In prayer, we escape the cares of the world and enjoy
the peace of God. In God's presence, stress melts away
and is replaced with an assurance that all will be okay.

With the peace of our souls restored, we become
focused on what is truly important. We return to our
activities with a commitment to God in all that we do.

> "The spirit of God has made me,
> and the breath of the Almighty
> gives me life."
> —Job 33:4

Day 231

---◆---

We invite joy into our life by keeping our thoughts on God.

OUR THOUGHTS

The thoughts we continually hold in mind directly and powerfully affect how we feel and act and what we experience. So we know to allow only the people and situations we want to invite into our life to occupy our thoughts.

We realize how important thoughts of joy are to our own well-being. With our thoughts, we invite more joy into our day and we recognize the people and things about which we are joyful.

Keeping our thoughts centered on the presence of God, we feel the celebration that is happening within our very thoughts. We know and express the joy of living.

As we let the joy of God inspire us and uplift us, we accept our Creator's help over the rough spots and onto the smooth, even pathways of life.

There is gladness within us that is reflected out into our life.

> "For they will scarcely brood over the days
> of their lives, because God keeps them occupied
> with the joy of their hearts."—Ecclesiastes 5:20

Day 232

———◆———

We can, because with God,
all things are possible for us.

WE CAN! At times when we thought we could not possibly complete a goal, we felt a stirring inside us that urged us to keep on, to trust that God was helping us all the way. And God did help us reach our goal!

With God, all things are possible, and knowing this we are able to push doubt aside and affirm with conviction: *We can! Yes, with God, we can!*

We believe in ourselves and in our own abilities because God is our inspiration and hope. God will never fail us, and we cannot fail when we hold to the belief that nothing is impossible for God and us.

The possibilities that do become reality may not be what we had envisioned they would be or even could be. Yet with God guiding us all the way, we are led to our right place and led in doing the right thing.

> "For mortals it is impossible,
> but for God all things are possible."
> —Matthew 19:26

Day 233

—◆—

*Loving each other is a powerful way
of encouraging each other throughout life.*

ENCOURAGED Observing the strength that first one of us than the other had during some of the most challenging times of our life, we were encouraged. Each time we were positive that there was a solution to a problem when there appeared to be none, we helped bring about the solution.

We both appreciate the encouragement we received from each other. By cooperating with each other, we did make it through these times as a loving, supportive couple.

Being loved by each other is one of the greatest encouragements we can receive. We love each other at all times—when we are at our best and when we are not. This is the kind of unconditional love that is divine in nature and is so powerful in encouraging us throughout our life.

> **"I have indeed received much joy
> and encouragement from your love."**
> —Philemon 1:7

Day 234

—◆—

*In quiet times of meditating on the presence of God,
we prepare ourselves for peaceful communication.*

LETTING OFF STEAM

As emotions build under stress, we may feel as if we are in a pressure-cooker situation. One of us is going to blow if we don't let off some steam!

Our way of letting off steam is not about having a shouting match. It's about letting our minds and bodies become still as we meditate on the presence of God that is within us and upholding us. And here is what we might experience:

Sitting in a comfortable chair in a quiet place, we close our eyes. Next we breathe in, inhaling deeply the air that surrounds us. As we release that breath of air, we also release all worry thoughts, all thoughts except the thought of God's presence.

Silently we invite the peace of God to move through our minds and bodies and relieve us of all stress. Yes, we are letting off steam and preparing ourselves for peaceful, meaningful communication with each other.

"A tranquil mind gives life to the flesh."
—Proverbs 14:30

Day 235

—◆—

Guided by the wisdom of God,
we are in our right place.

RIGHT PLACE The Wise Men of biblical times were guided to the right place by a brilliant star in the heavens. They did not let anyone or anything deter them from reaching the Child in the manger.

We also have a light to guide us so that we are in our right place to give and receive blessings. Our light shines from the spirit of God within us. Divine light is wisdom that reveals understanding, so that our plans include all that is needed to keep us thriving in an environment of love and life.

We understand much, but still there is more for us to understand. Led by the light of God, we will be in the right place to receive from and give back to life the riches of our Creator. We are living in the light of God, a sacred light of understanding that reveals all.

> "When they had heard the king, they set out;
> and there, ahead of them, went the star that they
> had seen at its rising, until it stopped over
> the place where the child was."
> —Matthew 2:9

Day 236

◆

*Today we experience the life, inspiration,
and peace of God.*

PROMISE OF TODAY

With confidence in God working through us, we declare that today is the day:

We are healed! We claim our healing even though we may not see evidence of it. The life of God within us is renewing and restoring us. Healing is continually happening within us, and our positive affirmations are an outer expression of our inner reality.

We meet our goals! Today is the day we continue to work toward the goals we have already established and to set new goals. We are enthusiastic about what we are accomplishing and what we are about to accomplish.

We enjoy peace of mind. Our peace of mind is established through our awareness of the presence of God. Today—all through the day—we take a few moments to acknowledge the presence of God and the blessing of peace that this realization brings us.

"His divine power has given us everything needed
for life and godliness. . . . Thus he has given us, through
these things, his precious and very great promises."
—2 Peter 1:3–4

DAILY WORD FOR COUPLES

Day 237
— ◆ —

*We recognize the beauty of Spirit
within a world of diversity.*

**BEAUTY
OF SPIRIT**

We have heard the saying that beauty is only skin-deep, yet we know there is a beauty that is truly spirit-deep. Within every human being is a beauty that only could have been created by God and sustained by the spirit of God.

We live in a world of diversity, a world in which—with all the different shapes and sizes, textures and colors, beliefs and understandings—no two people are exactly alike. Yet beneath the very different and unique outer appearances, the spirit of God resides. The spirit of God within us connects us with each other and with our family and friends. As two members of God's universal family, we share a beauty of Spirit that shines from us.

We recognize the beauty of Spirit within us and thank God for a world of diversity.

> **"In him was life, and the life
> was the light of all people."**
> **—John 1:4**

Day 238

—◆—

God has prepared us for today
and for every tomorrow.

PREPARED Half the fun of going on a trip or working on a project is planning for fun times and success. Yet we may not always have the luxury of spending time preparing for an upcoming event. So we trust that a beautiful mystery of life will unfold for us each day, and we prepare for it through our faith-filled prayers and actions.

The spirit of God within prepares us both mentally and physically, allowing us to meet each day with confidence. In the face of challenge, we stand firm in our faith, for God has prepared us for great possibilities.

Yes, we greet today and each tomorrow with courage and enthusiasm. God has prepared us for life, for we have strength, confidence, and peace of mind. We are prepared!

"The light is with you."
—John 12:35

Day 239

Our Prayer

Dear God,

We are praying for each other because of the love we feel in our hearts and also because we want to be supportive of each other in experiencing a life of health, understanding, and discovery.

We are complete and whole because Your spirit fills us with ever-renewing life. Our bodies are glorious designs of life and renewal. We have been created for life and created to be renewed with life.

There is nothing in the world that can defeat us because we are basing our decisions and actions on Your guidance. Life is a sacred experience. In every moment of our life, You are our ever-present guide.

Yes, we are praying because we have faith in You and in each other. And as we pray, we know that You are listening because You love us. We are being blessed by Your love in every moment.

"But truly God has listened; he has given heed to the words of my prayer."
—Psalms 66:19

Day 240

—◆—

My Gift to You

I GIVE YOU THE GIFT OF SHARING AN ENTHUSIASM FOR LIFE.

Looking up at the stars at night, watching them twinkle and glitter above us, it may seem as if we could reach out and touch them. Seeing this glorious blanket of glittering lights in the sky, we have no doubt about the glory and majesty of God.

And watching as the dawn begins to lighten the sky and magnificent colors dance across the horizon, we share an enthusiasm for life.

I pray that you will take this enthusiasm with you through the day. If we should be away from each other at any time, let's remember those twinkling stars and the colors of the dawn. These memories will bring us together in thought. Our enthusiasm for life and for living fills the time, and soon we will be with each other again.

> **"By the tender mercy of our God,
> the dawn from on high will break upon us."
> —Luke 1:78**

OUR SILENT CHILD; OUR TEACHER

By Troylyn Ball

A few days after our son, Marshall, was born, my husband, Charlie, and I took our beautiful 8-pound baby home. At 2 months, he was below the range of normal weight for an infant his age. By the time he was 9 months old, we knew that something was wrong. He was still underweight and showed no interest in playing with his toys or even being aware of them.

Because of Marshall, Charlie and I have learned tremendous lessons in patience and wonder. From the beginning, we read to Marshall and talked to him as if he were listening to everything we said. We counted his fingers and toes aloud and sang the ABCs to him.

Over time, we discovered that Marshall could not speak, nor could he walk independently. We saw no indication that he was even listening until he was 3½. I was holding Marshall in my lap, trying to interest him in one of his toys when he leaned forward and with his head touched a button by the picture of cat that made a meow sound. When I asked him to touch the cat button again, he did. As, one by one, I called out the names of other animals pictured, Marshall touched the correct button.

Elated that he was listening, we gave him more to hear. We played tapes of music, books, and the Bible for Marshall and continued to read to him. Charlie and I worked together in teaching Marshall. We were a team, supporting each other. When one of us would feel down, the other was there to help lift the situation back up to a positive level. We focused on his loving qualities.

At age 4, Marshall was in the hospital with pneumonia that threatened to take his life. Several days into our vigil at Marshall's bedside, the doctor asked us to step outside Marshall's room to talk with him.

Although he was a kind man, his training as a doctor had taught him to be direct: "Marshall has been in a race for his life, and he is growing tired. It's as if he hasn't had time to stop and draw a deep breath that he needs to sustain him. You will need to make a decision if his condition continues to deteriorate, for he will be unable to breathe on his own. What do you want us to do or not do for him when this happens?"

We understood that the doctor was asking us about whether or not to put Marshall on life support. Charlie and I had prayed and prayed and tried to remain positive about Marshall's outcome, but the doctors who were checking Marshall's vital signs offered little or no hope. Our firstborn child had severe physical disabilities. He had never talked or walked, and we knew that once a child with such disabilities was placed on life support, he would most likely never come off.

We held on to hope as we told the doctor, "God is in control of Marshall—has been and is now. We will leave Marshall in God's hands."

We trusted that Marshall could be in no better place than God's hands, and God proved us right. Marshall continued to breathe on his own and overcame pneumonia.

He continued to learn also and was able to complete schoolwork by using his head to point to pictures or words that correctly answered each question.

At age 5, he began using an alphabet board. With one of us supporting his arm at the elbow, he was now able to point with his finger, spelling words. He wrote his first poem about God:

> *Altogether Lovely*
>
> *God is good and merciful*
> *because He is also bright and intelligent.*
> *Seeing, feeling all that is true.*
> *Clearly He feels and listens to all our desires.*
> *Clearly He has everybody's dreams in mind.*
> *I see a God altogether lovely.*

When Marshall was 9 years old, he tested above a 12th-grade reading comprehension level. Marshall's grandmother accompanied him to school as his aide. One day during class, his teacher explained that a third-grader in another class had died unexpectedly of brain trauma. Marshall wrote to the parents that night. The day after the mother received Marshall's letter, she came to school to thank the child who had written such a beautiful letter.

Marshall continues to write. A compilation of his thoughts, letters, and poems has been published in a book, *Kiss of God: The Wisdom of a Silent Child*. Marshall has touched the lives of many people through his book. He has a unique way of expressing himself in his writings. I believe he perceives the wonder of life and the presence of God intuitively, not because of what others have taught him. Although he remains a silent child, Marshall has taught us how to listen to him, and he is a great teacher.

Day 241

◆

*During a sacred retreat with God, we are one
with the love and peace of God.*

**SACRED
RETREAT**

Spending a day or more on a retreat
at a special place offers us rest from
whatever may be troubling or stressful.
A retreat can also be a short time of
contemplation on the sacred wherever we are. This is
something we do often by closing our eyes and
focusing our attention on the spirit of God.

Our Creator always has time for us, so at any time,
we can take a break from our work or activity to be one
with the presence of God. We immediately feel at peace
with ourselves and with our surroundings.

A sacred retreat takes us away from adverse
situations and prepares us to spend time resting in the
love and peace of God. We welcome these interludes,
for they help us realize that we are always one with the
love and peace of God.

> "When you search for me,
> you will find me."
> —Jeremiah 29:13

Day 242

---◆---

*We are willing to open ourselves and our life
to the inspiration of God.*

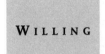

WILLING

In a desire to make progress in our personal life or in our careers, we have been willing to try to accomplish things we may have questioned whether or not we could accomplish and to allow ourselves to make mistakes.

Because we are willing to explore the unfamiliar, we did learn from our achievements and mistakes. We now realize that the times we prayed and searched our souls to discover what we needed to do in a crisis served as some of our most helpful lessons in life.

They were not easy times; however, God was our inspiration in bringing our thinking and feelings up to a positive level. Then we were able to move forward and really make progress in something that was important to us. We are more than willing to open ourselves and our life to the inspiration of God.

> **"Restore to me the joy of your salvation,
> and sustain in me a willing spirit."**
> **—Psalms 51:12**

Day 243

—◆—

The wisdom and power
of God's spirit shine from us.

INNER REALITY

Watching television or reading magazines and books, we may feel inundated with information about programs and products that could improve our appearances.

Appearance is important; yet, there is more to us than what can be seen on the outside. It's true: The spirit of God is at the core of our beings. This is an inner reality that is essential to our spiritual, physical, and emotional well-being.

As we let the wisdom and power of God's spirit within us be a part of what we think, say, and do, we are thinking, speaking, and acting from our divine nature. We shine the light of divine understanding on our relationship.

What an honor and a joy it is for us to express the goodness of God.

> "Do you not know that your body is
> a temple of the Holy Spirit within you,
> which you have from God?"
> —1 Corinthians 6:19

Day 244

*We give thanks for God's love, a treasure
of our hearts and souls.*

**LOVE
IS A
TREASURE**

We have collected many treasures
throughout our life together. Cards and
letters from loved ones touch our
hearts each time we read them.
Achievements and experiences fortify our confidence
each time we think about them. Times of being totally
in the presence of our Creator nourish our souls each
time we experience them.

The treasures we value most are ones that cause us to
remember how the love of God moves in and through
other people, situations, and us. God is expressing love
through us, our family and friends, and the events of
each day.

There is a wealth of treasure to behold, accept, and
enjoy every day, because God is constantly pouring out
love to us and through us. We thank God that we are
loved and that we are loving.

> "Whoever obeys his word,
> truly in this person the love of God
> has reached perfection."
> —1 John 2:5

Day 245

---◆---

*We discover so much to be thankful for
each time we count our blessings.*

**COUNTING
OUR
BLESSINGS**   When our world seems to turn
upside down because of some
challenge, we can help turn it right side
up by counting our blessings.

The more blessings we bring to mind, the more we
realize that so many good things are happening in our
life. The blessings of loved ones, pets, and our home
outweigh the challenges of leaky plumbing or a broken
appliance.

What seemed like a topsy-turvy world was really
caused by a distorted view of it. Looking for the good,
we discover it everywhere. Sometimes what we had
considered to be a challenge turns out to be a chance
for us to express strengths and a creativity we never
realized we had. That is a blessing!

**"Happy are the people to whom such blessings fall;
happy are the people whose God is the Lord."
—Psalms 144:15**

Day 246

---◆---

*Through the presence of God within, we are forever one
with our children.*

**ONE
WITH OUR
CHILDREN**
A home that was once full of the
laughter and activity of children may
seem too quiet when the children have
grown up and gone out on their own.
We may long for the times when we had to say, "Quiet
down!" or "Time for bed!"

The quiet we desired in the past may seem to evoke
an empty feeling within us now. We are still parents
who love and care about our children, but we know
that letting them experience a life of their own is what
they need to do.

We take great comfort in knowing that God is with
them, guiding and protecting them. Through the
presence of God, we are forever one with them. How
good it is to welcome them back into our home and our
life for a visit. In the meantime, they are always in our
thoughts and our prayers.

"They shall not labor in vain,
or bear children for calamity;
for they shall be offspring blessed by the Lord."
—Isaiah 65:23

Day 247

—◆—

We have the kind of confidence that is founded on our faith in God.

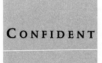

CONFIDENT

With great love and caring, God has brought us to this day, to this moment, and we accept both the responsibilities and the blessings of being who we are: creations of God.

When so much is happening at such a fast pace, we do not become anxious. Our faith in God calms us and relieves us of stressful feelings. We know that wherever we are, whatever the situation may be, God is with us. Wherever we may go, the spirit of God goes before us and also accompanies us all the way.

Others may or may not agree with our choices, yet we live our life as confident people. Our confidence comes from our faith in God concerning all matters and an understanding that God is working through us to bring about the best outcomes.

**"Jesus answered them,
'Have faith in God.'"
—Mark 11:22**

Day 248

—◆—

*In speaking God's name, we are saying
a prayer of protection.*

PROTECTED
Just saying God's name helps us realize that God is our constant guide and companion.

We feel the magnitude of God's power and the assurance of God's sacred presence in prayer no matter how brief a prayer may be. While driving through a maze of heavy traffic, we may both whisper God's name: "God . . . God . . . God," helping whichever one of us who is driving to remain calm and alert.

In speaking God's name, we are saying a prayer that helps us make a conscious connection with God's presence in all situations. God guides us so that we know what to do for our own well-being and how to be considerate of the well-being of others.

Thank God for providing us with strength of body and soul.

"The name of the Lord is a strong tower;
the righteous run into it and are safe."
—Proverbs 18:10

DAILY WORD FOR COUPLES

Day 249

*We are working in partnership
with each other and with God.*

OPEN

It is not the length of time that we have known each other that guarantees that our relationship is an open one. Because of our love for and our willingness to cooperate with each other, we remain approachable and honest with each other.

Because we are taking the time to learn more about each other and basing this relationship on a firm foundation of our awareness of God, we are friends and confidants. We can say anything that is on our minds and know that we will listen with genuine interest and concern. Because we are open about our feelings, we can overcome and even avoid problems.

We are open and honest with each other, knowing that our love for each other is strong. How blessed we feel knowing that we are living and working in partnership with each other and with God to continually make our relationship stronger.

"And the peace of God, which surpasses all understanding, will guard your hearts and your minds."
—Philippians 4:7

Day 250

---◆---

*We are children of God whose cheerful hearts
are reflected in all that we do.*

CHEERFUL HEARTS A cheerful heart boosts our spirits and adds to our confidence in ourselves. We are able to see that there is a bright side to a situation and to share that vision with each other. Being cheerful, we are relieved of tension and filled with a zest for living.

Our true happiness is an inner quality of our spiritual heritage. Aware of this, we allow the joy within us to flow out into our conversations and into whatever projects we are working on. We are happy being who we are—children of God who are fulfilled in our personal relationship with the Creator.

We greet everyone with a smile, and every smile is an outer celebration inspired by our cheerful hearts. We gratefully acknowledge that God is the source of our enthusiasm for life and the source of the cheerfulness that we feel in our hearts and reflect in everyday living.

> "Do not lag in zeal, be ardent
> in spirit, serve the Lord."
> —Romans 12:11

Day 251

*Filled with the life of God, we are also filled
with energy. We have strength of mind and body.*

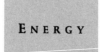

ENERGY God energizes the cells of our
bodies with life. So if we are facing a
task today that requires an extra
measure of strength and endurance,
we can and do rely on the life of God within us.

First, we rest in a realization of our strength as we
affirm: *Filled with the life of God, I have the strength to do
whatever needs to be done by me.*

The power of God flows through us as energy and
fortitude. Filled with divine energy, we have strength
and we have the wisdom to use it in productive activity.

Strength of mind is revealed in our ability to think
clearly and to respond appropriately. Innovative
thoughts awaken us to a world of possibilities.

> "In returning and rest you shall be saved;
> in quietness and in trust shall be your strength."
> —Isaiah 30:15

Day 252

—◆—

*We agree that God is our source
of wisdom and love.*

AGREE Our individual views and opinions do differ occasionally, yet we honor each other's freedom of expression. Encouraging each other to give expression to our thoughts, we have interesting, stimulating conversations.

Because we agree that we can disagree and still be a loving couple, we enjoy being with each other. There is a freshness in our relationship that allows us to discover more about each other every day.

There is so much more that we agree on than we disagree about, and when there is a disagreement that concerns us, we pray about it. God is our source of wisdom and love. United in prayer, we bring a solidarity to our relationship that enriches our life and keeps us moving in a positive direction.

> "Again, truly I tell you, if two of you agree
> on earth about anything you ask, it will be done
> for you by my father in heaven."
> —Matthew 18:19

Day 253

—◆—

We accept each new opportunity to learn
as we move toward our goals.

ANOTHER CHANCE Young children learning to walk usually fall several times as they work at gaining enough balance to take a few steps. Yet they are so eager to have another chance—again and again—that they do learn to walk and then eventually to run!

As adults we, too, may stumble when we are learning something new. Yet we know that God will give us another chance. The timing and degree of our success will be different from what others experience, and this is okay. We have faith in God and an eagerness to learn.

We may or may not reach our goal today, but tomorrow holds new promise and possibility. With just one more day, one more time of trying, we realize a breakthrough to new understanding.

> "So if anyone is in Christ, there is a new creation:
> everything old has passed away; see,
> everything has become new!"
> —2 Corinthians 5:17

Day 254

Our Prayer

Dear God,

   We feel an incredible peace move through us as we pray for ourselves and each other in the solitude of a quiet, comfortable place. Alone with You in prayer and thinking loving thoughts about each other, we experience a satisfaction of the soul.

   In that quiet time, we link our hearts in prayer. Praying for each other, we realize the power for good that is being generated by us and for us.

   God, with You to guide our way, we do make a powerful, positive difference in our life and in our relationship with each other. We pray from a heart of love, saturating the very atmosphere with loving thoughts. What rejoicing takes place when our hearts are linked in prayer!

> "Our heart is glad in him,
> because we trust in his holy name.
> Let your steadfast love, O Lord, be upon us,
> even as we hope in you."
> —Psalms 33:21–22

Day 255

———— ♦ ————

My Gift to You

I GIVE YOU THE GIFT
OF QUALITY TIME.

I have a gift for you today. It's not an expensive one,
nor is it wrapped in colorful paper. It is something that
can seem to slip through our fingers when we try to
grab hold of it, but when we do put each other first, it
happens so effortlessly.

My gift to you is quality time. This means I am here
for you in every way. The time I spend with you
includes my love, attention, consideration, and so much
more. With all distractions aside, I listen to you and talk
to you.

I know that you feel the same way I do: The greatest
quality time we can give to each other is to pray for
each other and pray together. We also can be quiet,
listen to our favorite music, or walk hand in hand.

I thank God for you, and concentrating on you is
meaningful to me and honors you as my partner and
my best friend.

"O magnify the Lord with me,
and let us exalt his name together."
—Psalms 34:3

Day 256

❖

With faith-filled hearts and renewed enthusiasm,
we begin again.

BEGINNING AGAIN Has some kind of change brought us to a crossroad of life? Changes in us and in our life may lead us in a new direction or along an unfamiliar path.

The good news is that whenever we reach one of these crossroads, we have an opportunity for a fresh start. We can begin again.

The mistakes of the past serve as lessons in what we can do differently or improve doing. Life is change, and change requires growth on our part. As we continue to make new beginnings in our life, we flow with change. With each new beginning, we are becoming so much more—more loving, more faith-filled, and more spiritually enriched.

This day is a new beginning for us, and we embrace it with enthusiasm.

> "Sing to him a new song; play skillfully
> on the strings, with loud shouts."
> —Psalms 33:3

DAILY WORD FOR COUPLES

Day 257

---◆---

*Divine understanding is the guiding light
of our life.*

**GUIDING
LIGHT**

The beacon of a lighthouse during fog or a storm is a welcome source of guidance to the crew of a ship, alerting them to nearby rocks and the shoreline.
The spirit of God within is a spiritual beacon that we look to for guidance each day with every decision we make. Like that lighthouse beacon, God reveals the way around obstacles. God inspires us with ideas that help us make wise choices.

With God's help, we are moving ahead in life and we are keeping our focus on what we desire to accomplish. With every decision we make, we are following where the light of God leads us. The blessed assurance of God comforts us if we ever feel discouraged and encourages us to remember that divine light is shining within us and before us—always.

> "From there you will seek the Lord your God,
> and you will find him if you search after him
> with all your heart and soul."
> —Deuteronomy 4:29

Day 258

---◆---

*Expressing our spirituality, we give more
in life and receive more from life.*

A FULLER LIFE   Our giving more in life rather than getting more from life is what builds a fuller, more fulfilling life for us. We believe what we are giving is the love, compassion, and understanding of God that are within us waiting to be expressed.

The movement of God's spirit from within us out into our words and actions is an expression of our spirituality. When we are fully experiencing the reality of our spiritual nature, our life is indeed full—full with the presence of God and full with the expression of the sacred attributes that God's spirit within has given us.

We are living from our inner spiritual nature, giving more in life and receiving more from life—every day.

> **"The measure you give will be
> the measure you get back."**
> **—Luke 6:38**

Day 259

◆

Thank God for animal friends.

OUR PETS Sharing our life with a pet is a decision we do not make hastily. Before bringing an animal into our home, we consider all the responsibilities that come with it. This is one of God's creatures, and we want to give it the time and attention it deserves.

God has created a tremendous variety of animals, and each one has its own traits and personality. In considering a new pet, we ask ourselves if our home and yard provide a safe environment for this animal. Will this pet fit in as a member of our family? We ask God to guide us in making our decision.

We will be sharing our home and our hearts with this pet. Gazing into its eyes, we see life and love sparkling there. We recognize our pet as a friend and companion that is ready, willing, and able to share its love and affection with us. What a gift our pet is!

> "So God created . . . every living creature. . . .
> And God saw that it was good."
> —Genesis 1:21

Day 260

♦

*In the silence of prayer, we are blessed
with messages of life and peace.*

**DIVINE
MESSAGE**
When we talk on the telephone to friends and loved ones who are thousands of miles away, we are amazed at how clear their voices sound. If we close our eyes, we can imagine that they are in the same room with us.

The voice of God comes to us in clear messages as well. When we close our eyes and enter into a prayerful state, we truly experience God. Divinely inspired thoughts come to us in our time of meditation. It's as though God has taken us by the hand and is speaking to us gently and lovingly in a language of the soul.

Waves of peace surge through us as we take each message from God into our minds and our hearts. These messages play back to us as wisdom that guides us in daily living.

"This is the message we have heard from him
and proclaim to you, that God is light and in him
there is no darkness at all."
—1 John 1:5

Day 261

---◆---

*God's loving, powerful spirit moves through us
as spiritual freedom.*

**SPIRITUAL
FREEDOM**

To an observer, some situations and
conditions may appear to limit us; we
know, however, that our freedom is
never limited, for it is freedom of Spirit.

If we are working in an environment where absolute
quiet must be observed, we can turn up the volume of a
song of joy that is playing within us and still not disturb
others. If we are in a noisy environment, we can escape
for a few minutes by taking a spiritual break, a peaceful
time of prayer and meditation right where we are.

God's loving, powerful spirit moves through us as
spiritual freedom that blesses us and enables us to bless
others. We are free to go the extra mile in helping
others—not because we have to, but because it is a way
of expressing our spiritual freedom and benefiting the
family of God.

> **"I delight to do your will, O my God;
> your law is within my heart."**
> **—Psalms 40:8**

Day 262

—◆—

*Today is the day we say and do
what comes from our hearts of love.*

**HEARTS
OF LOVE**

When one or both of us have left an "I love you" unsaid or a situation unresolved, we are putting off something that may be vital to the goodwill of our relationship. Chances are we may put off the unsaid and unresolved again and again.

Yet when we express love and do what we can to correct a misunderstanding, we are relieved and no longer have regrets. As we invite God's love to flow through our words and actions, we help bring about a reconciliation between us.

Today is a good day to say what is from our hearts of love, a day for expressing and accepting forgiveness and understanding. Today is the day to make amends, to bond with each other in spiritual unity.

> "Your light shall break forth
> like the dawn."
> —Isaiah 58:8

Day 263

—◆—

*Our optimism is a declaration
of our faith in God.*

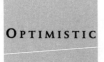

OPTIMISTIC

Being optimists, we expect the best to happen. We know that our positive expectations brighten even the dreariest of days for us, and we hope that our optimism helps brighten the days for others.

From where do we draw such an upbeat attitude? We believe our faith is the source of our optimism. Faith in God inspires us to expect the best and also to do our best.

Then we are able to perceive all in the light of faith: God is present in every situation and circumstance, and in the presence of God, there is no limit to the good that can happen and that will happen.

Optimism is revealed in our smiles, the joy-filled lilt in our voices, the positiveness of our thoughts—all are declarations of our faith in God.

> **"When Jesus heard him, he was amazed and said
> to those who followed him, 'Truly I tell you,
> in no one in Israel have I found such faith.'"**
> **—Matthew 8:10**

Day 264

—◆—

Aware of God's presence,
we are relaxed and confident.

RELAX

On occasion, we may be so keyed up with excitement that we are unable to relax. Although we are not physically active, our minds are racing ahead, pondering all kinds of possibilities.

To truly relax, not just our bodies but our minds as well, we take deep breaths and clear our minds of every thought except the thought of God's presence within us and around us.

Experiencing the presence of God, we do relax. Our heart rates stabilize and our breathing becomes steady. Relaxed and confident, we then make a fresh start with our day and with our plans.

We are living life moment by moment and enjoying the blessing that each moment truly is.

"Return, O my soul, to your rest,
for the Lord has dealt bountifully with you."
—Psalms 116:7

Day 265

*We recognize that every day is an occasion
for celebrating God's glory, and we do.*

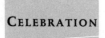

CELEBRATION

Special occasions are cause for celebration, and we enjoy each opportunity to express our heartfelt joy. Yet whenever we pause to consider the gift from God that each day is, we have reason to celebrate the joy and splendor of God every day.

Our celebration is not a loud, flamboyant one; it is a quiet, consecrated time of experiencing God's presence. We express a joy of the soul that is naturally reflected in our conversations and activities.

It has been said that the eyes are the windows to the soul, and we trust that everyone who looks into our eyes will see the joy of God's spirit there.

With everything that we do or say, we celebrate the spirit of God that dwells within us.

> **"For you shall go out in joy,
> and be led back in peace."**
> **—Isaiah 55:12**

Day 266

—◆—

As we give thanks to God for blessing us,
we are reminded of how blessed we are.

HOW BLESSED WE ARE As we pay our bills each month, we are thankful that we have the money to pay them. Both of us are especially thankful when there is money left over in our bank account after we have paid our bills!

In prayer, we seek the answers we need concerning our financial situation and changes that might affect the quality of our life. God has been, is now, and will always be the source of our prosperity. Relying on the wisdom of God to guide our words and actions, we are blessed in financial matters as well as those involving our health and relationship.

Many blessings contribute to our prosperity, and each time we give thanks to God, we are reminded of how prosperous we are.

"The Lord bless you and keep you;
the Lord make his face to shine upon you,
and be gracious to you;
the Lord lift up his countenance upon you,
and give you peace."
—Numbers 6:24–26

Day 267

---◆---

Each day, we answer
a wake-up call to Spirit.

SPIRITUAL AWAKENING
We have come far in our relationship with God and our understanding of our own spiritual nature.

Knowing God and our spiritual identity, we have been able to make positive changes in the way we think, speak, and act—all of which have blessed us.

At one time we may have questioned our faith, but we have had a spiritual awakening. Our faith is strong, and we are continuing to grow in spiritual awareness. Each day we answer a wake-up call to learn more about God and ourselves. Each day, we are richer in spiritual awareness and understanding than we were the day before. This is because we awaken more fully to Spirit each day.

> "Awake, my soul!
> Awake, O harp and lyre!
> I will awake the dawn.
> I will give thanks to you, O Lord."
> —Psalms 57:8–9

Day 268

—◆—

*A sense of humor lightens and brightens
our view of life.*

SENSE OF HUMOR
Thank God that we do have a sense of humor that allows us to see through a mist of confusion to the celebration of life that is sparkling in all creation.

Looking at a situation with a sense of humor helps. Our attitudes become lighter and brighter. Then we are able to perceive that a disagreement between us or between one of us and another person is a misunderstanding. We are encouraged to keep our lines of communication open so that our relationships are kept intact.

With the God-given qualities of imagination and understanding, we do have a sense of humor that blesses us and blesses the people in our home and work environments. As we talk and laugh with others, we are expressing a joy that moves out from the depths of our souls and touches others with gladness.

> "He will yet fill your mouth with laughter,
> and your lips with shouts of joy."
> —Job 8:21

Day 269

Our Prayer

Dear God,

Within a time of quiet inner reflection, we experience a few moments of divine clarity, a time in which we are totally aware of You and feel Your presence in every ounce of our being.

During this sacred connection with You, we realize a simple, powerful truth—our awareness of You is all important to us. With this realization, we know that keeping up with the hustle and bustle of the day is not what is crucial to our well-being. What truly matters is our relationship with You, and in this moment we realize our oneness with You.

Experiencing this sacred connection, we are energized. We are one with Your eternal life and wisdom. From this moment on, we will live our life from this truth.

> "Listen to the sound of my cry,
> my King and my God,
> for to you I pray."
> —Psalms 5:2

Day 270

◆

My Gift to You

**I GIVE YOU THE GIFT
OF MY INFINITE TRUST.**

Trust is a priceless gift of love. I give you the gift of my trust as an expression of my love for you.

Knowing that trust can be a fragile thing—easily broken and difficult to replace—we both treat it with the respect that it deserves. You or I would never do anything to betray our trust in each other, for our trust emanates from our love for each other.

Trust and respect go hand in hand. I trust you because I believe in you—in your kindness, in your gentle nature, in your love for God and for me.

I have faith in you to stand by me, come what may, for I believe with all my heart and soul that God is watching over our relationship and guiding us in every moment.

Today and every day, I give you the gift of my trust.

"Let me hear of your steadfast love
in the morning, for in you I put my trust."
—Psalms 143:8

WORTHY OF LOVE

BY DAVE PELZER

People have asked how I could ever be in a meaningful relationship with a woman after a childhood of being brutally abused by my mother. Often our mothers are the pattern by which we relate to all women. My first marriage did end in divorce, but from that marriage I was given one of my best and dearest friends—my son, Stephen.

As a child, I longed for my parents' love. They were both alcoholics, and after my father left our family, my mother turned her rage on one of their four sons. I happened to be that one.

My mother constantly blamed me for "messing up" and referred to me as "It." Her anger increased over the next few years as she hit me and denied me food. When I was 8 years old, she punished me by holding my arm over the burning flames of our kitchen stove.

Eventually I was so badly abused by her that I could no longer explain away the bruises on my face and body to my teachers or school nurse. At the age of 12, I was taken out of my home and placed in foster care.

My second wife, Marsha, was the first person to say, "God loves you, Dave. I love you too, and I believe in you!" Hearing those words, I started crying uncontrollably. I felt the joy of being loved. This wonderful woman loved *me*—a man who for much of his life felt that he was unworthy of love.

Marsha and I began in a working relationship—at a distance. I lived in California, and she lived in Florida. She was working as the editor of a book I had written, and we talked over the phone daily. I began to open up to her in ways I had never been able to open up to any other person. We took baby steps in building a friendship and in building our trust in each other.

We met for the first time when I invited her to California. Ready to test the waters, we wanted to know if there was a possibility for more than friendship between us. I met Marsha at the airport, holding a single yellow rose. She later told me that her heart was pounding so that she thought she was going to pass out. When she saw me, everything and everyone else faded away. She said right then and there, "This is the man I'm going to marry!"

She was right. Marsha left her parents, friends, and everything and moved to California. We married and she became the director of a company that I had just started. Our marriage was tested, because the money just wasn't there in the beginning. We placed ourselves and our lives in God's hands. Once the books started selling, we actually had an income.

My message in my books and in my talks is about resilience and responsibility. Many people have had tremendous issues in their past, but they have been resilient and responsible enough to leapfrog over them.

True, I was abused as a child. My mother would not let me speak at home, so I mumbled. Being resilient and taking the responsibility for my own life, I have written three best-selling books and I speak to audiences all over the country. I have learned Japanese and Russian and I do stand-up comedy. Yet I believe in simply focusing on doing the best job I can do. My job is helping others know that they can turn their lives around also.

I check in with myself every day, praying that I am doing the right thing for the right reasons. I wish I could discover the cure for cancer or find a way to feed all the people of the world, but what I do is bring a message of resilience and responsibility to the arena of child abuse.

Parents come up to me at book signings and lectures and tell me that, after reading my book *A Child Called "It"*, they can't wait to give their kids a hug. Teenagers tell me that when they put the book down, they immediately go to their parents and say, "Mom, Dad, I love you! And I am going to clean up my room."

When I received the TOYA—the Ten Outstanding

Young Americans Award (the equivalent of an Oscar for good samaritans)—I walked onto a stage in front of over 2,500 people and didn't know what to say. Someone had suggested that I accept the award using my flair for comedy by doing my impression of former president Bush. When I opened my mouth to speak, however, I spoke from my heart as *me*. And something like this came out:

"Ladies and gentlemen, I would be sorely remiss if I did not pay homage to the people who played such a vital role in my life. I wish to dedicate this award to my grade-school principal, teachers, and nurse, all who, on March 5, 1973, intervened and saved me from further harm. They risked their jobs, their livelihoods, by speaking out to authorities about my abuse. They saved my life.

"I also want to dedicate this award to my social workers, who stood by me even though—just hours before going to court—I recanted every statement I had made about being abused by my mother. I want to recognize my foster parents, who taught me how to walk and to talk and encouraged me to be the best person I could be.

"If it were not for these people, only God knows where I would be today. People make a difference. And with that, ladies and gentlemen, let's observe a moment of silence and thank God for who we are and what we have, right now today."

I had not planned to say all this, and I felt as if God had given me a message to share. After a moment of silence, I walked out of the spotlight and off the stage. The audience remained silent. Then there was thunderous applause. I knew they had heard the message: We can all make a positive difference in the lives of children.

I look back at my mom and our relationship and recognize it as the tragedy it was. I don't believe that people wake up one morning and decide to be alcoholics. Neither do loving, caring parents suddenly decide to beat their children. Desperate acts such as these are something that leaches out of people because of their unresolved issues.

My mom obviously had some unresolved issues that showed up in her as alcoholism, frustration, and anger. Often child abuse is passed down from one generation to another, but I decided to leave this planet cleaner than I found it in my own childhood. I think we all have responsibilities as parents, spouses, and members of humanity. I carried the cross of abuse during my childhood, but my son did not have to experience what I did.

Being resilient and answering the wake-up call to responsibility, I learned that I can have close relationships and that I am worthy of love. My wife and son are living proof of that!

Day 271

—◆—

We prepare for each day
by beginning each day with prayer.

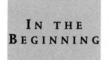

IN THE BEGINNING Although we are moving into the unknown, each new beginning holds the promise of blessings that are awaiting our discovery.

Whether we are beginning to move our way through a challenge or to move forward with an opportunity, we have faith that God is leading us toward the right outcome.

There is so much promise in the beginning of a relationship, and we help keep that promise alive as we do our part in being the best friends we know how to be. And beyond our best, God is there to let us know how we can be even better friends.

Every day is a new beginning, and we begin each day in prayer with God.

"In the beginning when God created the heavens
and the earth, the earth was a formless void and darkness
covered the face of the deep."
—Genesis 1:1–2

DAILY WORD FOR COUPLES

Day 272

—◆—

The peace of God is radiating
within our souls.

MESSAGE OF PEACE Talking is one way we communicate our thoughts to each other. We also hear what we ourselves say. When we speak peaceful words, we broadcast a message of peace that vibrates throughout our minds and bodies. We are sending the message "Be at peace" to ourselves.

The peace of God is radiating within our souls. As we open our minds to divine peace, we are aware of how calm we can be—even during a crisis. We think clearly and act responsibly.

Filling our minds with thoughts of peace brings us so much relief, for it invites the peace of God to flow unimpeded throughout our beings.

> "Incline your ear and hear my words,
> and apply your mind to my teaching;
> for it will be pleasant if you keep
> them within you."
> —Proverbs 22:17–18

Day 273

— ◆ —

*Every breath we take refreshes
and renews us.*

**BREATH
OF
LIFE**

Taking a deep, cleansing breath is a simple yet effective way to refresh our bodies and our minds when we feel stressed.

As we breathe in slowly, we expand our lungs with fresh air and realize how alive we are! Holding that breath for a few seconds, we feel as if our bodies are tingling with health and vitality. We breathe out slowly and steadily, giving thanks to God for our lungs and the renewing work they do.

Drawing in another slow, deep breath, we experience clarity of mind. With each breath, we think about the life within us and how we are nurturing that life with oxygen-rich air and our positive thoughts.

After a few moments of steady, slow breathing, we are both relaxed and invigorated. We are alive with the breath of God.

"Then the Lord God formed man from the dust
of the ground, and breathed into his nostrils
the breath of life; and the man became a living being."
—Genesis 2:7

Day 274

___◆___

Faith calls us back again and again
to sacred communion with God.

SACRED COMMUNION Common sense and experience tell us not to wait to eat until we are weak from lack of food. We know that eating three nutritious meals a day helps us remain physically strong.

Wisdom of divine origin flows from God's spirit within us, encouraging us to keep prayed up so that we nourish our faith daily. Then our faith is strong and supports us through even the most serious time.

Faith in God prepares us to recognize and accept the blessings that God has ready for us. Faith calls us back again and again in sacred communion with God. Alone with God in thought and prayer, we are nourished. We have a hope that is built on the solid foundation of our faith in God. And God will never fail us.

"I will strengthen you,
I will help you."
—Isaiah 41:10

Day 275

*Change is an opportunity for us
to experience new adventures.*

**SIMPLE
STEPS**

When we are going through any kind of change, we help each other adjust by remembering the familiar adage that a journey of a thousand miles begins with a single step. So we think of change in single steps, one day at a time, rather than in a whole course of events. We are confident, for God is constantly guiding us and giving us the inner strength we need to face change with a sense of adventure.

We know that change is a necessary part of life and we rely on God to show us which change offers us an opportunity to make a positive difference in our life. We are eager to begin exploring the wonder that change is ready to reveal to us. Life is an adventure in which we eagerly participate.

> "Then the Lord answered me and said: . . .
> There is still a vision for the appointed time. . . .
> If it seems to tarry, wait for it;
> it will surely come, it will not delay."
> —Habakkuk 2:2–3

Day 276

God is preparing our way as order is restored and hope is revealed.

MOMENT OF CLARITY
There is a divine order at work that enables our life to unfold in ways that are beyond our greatest expectations.

In a moment of clarity, we realize that we are in the flow of divine order. Confusion lifts and we have greater understanding. Yes, we know what to do to meet our responsibilities to each other, our family, and our jobs and still pursue our own special interests.

God is preparing our way as divine order moves through our life and circumstances. Order is restored where there seemed to be chaos. Hope is revealed where there seemed to be none.

Because the order of God is always active, we are blessed by divine order every day.

"I will establish my covenant between me and you,
and your offspring after you throughout
their generations, for an everlasting covenant,
to be God to you and to your offspring after you."
—Genesis 17:7

Day 277

—◆—

Thought by thought, we help shape
great possibilities into reality.

IMAGINE THAT! Imagination is a powerful activity of the mind that takes place when our thoughts are open to divine ideas. Then we help bring great possibilities into reality.

We can imagine Jesus looking over the crowds of people who had come to Him to be healed. We hear the words of life and healing that Jesus spoke: "The blind receive their sight, the lame walk, the lepers are cleansed, the deaf hear, the dead are raised, and the poor have good news brought to them." (Matthew 11:4–5)

Thought by thought, word by word, we, too, shape our experiences. We use the power of our imagination to picture healing, prosperity, and peace. We hold positive images in mind and let our faith in God nourish them.

Yes, we do behold the goodness of God!

> **"I believe that I shall see the goodness of the Lord**
> **in the land of the living."**
> **—Psalms 27:13**

Day 278

---◆---

*Words of light reveal the truth
of life and healing.*

**WORDS
OF LIGHT**

As the rising sun casts its light over a flower garden, a spectacular array of colors, shapes, and textures bursts on the scene. Nothing really has changed in the garden, but light reveals the truth about flowers that were once shrouded in darkness.

Words of light reveal truth also. Each divine idea that we affirm shines the light of truth into our life and the lives of those around us.

Affirming that the life of God within us is renewing us, we are shining the light of healing within us. Every word of life and healing sends a message of renewal throughout our bodies.

We are not only willing, we are eager to let the truth of God's ever-renewing life shine through our words and our actions. Divine light reveals life and renewal.

> "As the Lord lives, whatever my God says,
> that I will speak."
> —2 Chronicles 18:13

Day 279

—◆—

God is our source of wisdom, a wisdom
that sustains us and guides us.

ONE DAY AT A TIME We are naturally curious about what could happen to us and through us in the future. Realistically, however, we can live only one day at a time.

So when we pray, we open ourselves and our life to the wisdom of God. We realize that we don't have to know what the future holds, for God is leading us so that we are prepared for life today and in every new day.

We have dreams and plans, but we are flexible enough not to limit ourselves and others by what we believe can be done. With God guiding us, we realize that every day is full of possibility. God is our reality in every moment, the source of wisdom and understanding that sustains us and guides us.

> "When the Spirit of truth comes, he will guide you into all the truth; for he will not speak on his own, but will speak whatever he hears, and he will declare to you the things that are to come."
> —John 16:13

Day 280

—◆—

When we pass along acts of kindness,
we reflect the sunshine of joy to others.

PASS IT ALONG In an instant, our day can brighten. When we give each other a smile, a kind comment, or show some other consideration, we are doing something that seems to bring the sun out from behind the clouds. We uplift each other.

We pass along the sunshine of our day by continuing to be kind to each other and by being kind to others. Like the Good Samaritan—who helped an injured stranger traveling to Jericho by doing all that he could for him with no thought of compensation—we treat everyone as we would like to be treated.

So we greet each other and our family with hugs and words of love. If a coworker seems to be having a difficult day, we offer words of encouragement. With a friendly smile to a store clerk, we show that we care. When we pass along acts of kindness, we reflect the sunshine of joy to others.

"Jesus said to him,
'Go and do likewise.'"
—Luke 10:37

Day 281

—◆—

God is the peace that fills our souls
in life's journey.

We may take frequent trips down memory lane, reviewing events of our life. Most memories are pleasant ones, but even those that are not pleasant cannot harm us now. We feel at peace about how far we have come in our growth and understanding.

We are at ease when we recall the past, for we have found the peace of God within us and have invited it to live out through us. In our heart of hearts, we know that God is not only the power that guides us along in our life's journey but also the love that uplifts us at all times.

God's spirit within is peace that permeates our entire beings, and we have confidence in ourselves. Wherever we are today in our journey, we have made progress from yesterday. We are in close communication with God as we move forward in life.

> "All the ends of the earth shall remember
> and turn to the Lord;
> and all the families of the nations
> shall worship before him."
> —Psalms 22:27

Day 282

—◆—

*As we apply divine wisdom in our life,
we make tremendous breakthroughs.*

**BREAK-
THROUGH**

While intently working at trying to solve a problem, we may be so focused on the problem that we miss discovering the solution.

When we give our full attention to God rather than the problem, we find that the answer does come. With God's help, we have made a breakthrough!

Our whole life goes so much more smoothly when we work in partnership with God. We have breakthroughs that transform difficult tasks into manageable ones. We give ourselves a break when we look to God for a breakthrough.

God is all wise and all knowing. We know what positive results happen when we remain focused on God—not merely when we seem to be at an impasse, but at all times. By applying divine wisdom in our life, we have true peace of mind.

> **"My mouth shall speak wisdom; the meditation
> of my heart shall be understanding."**
> **—Psalms 49:3**

Day 283

—◆—

Our every thought of God is a divine connection
with our Creator.

DIVINE CONNECTION

There is a world of difference between being alone and being lonely. We both enjoy times with family and friends, yet time alone with God revives our souls.

We may simply find a quiet place away from the activity of the day and sit in silence, with no other thought than a thought of God. We may speak a Scripture, such as, "You are my God, and I will give thanks to you." (Psalms 118:28)

Whatever we decide to do or say, we can make a conscious connection with the spirit of God. This divine connection clears our minds of confusion. We can make a divine connection with God at any time—with a thought, with a prayer. In fact, the connection is always there because God is always with us. Our awareness of God brings us the peace of mind of knowing we are in God's presence.

> "You are my God, and I will give thanks to you;
> you are my God, I will extol you."
> —Psalms 118:28

Day 284

---◆---

Our Prayer

Dear God,

At times we may feel a bit down but don't know if a lack of energy and enthusiasm is of a physical or emotional nature.

Something remarkable happens when we pray to You: We recharge our spiritual batteries. We have energy and enthusiasm that surge from us to become a part of all that we think, say, and do. We enjoy completing projects and starting new ones. Our conversations sparkle with love and laughter.

Because we are charged spiritually, we continue to express life, love, and wisdom in positive, life-enriching ways. We have a zest for living, and we are fulfilled in whatever we do.

We know that we truly are whole and holy beings, inspired by You to live life fully and to give back to life generously.

"When they had prayed, the place in which they were gathered together was shaken; and they were all filled with the Holy Spirit and spoke the word of God with boldness."
—Acts 4:31

Day 285

——◆——

My Gift to You

Gifted writers have the ability to weave words together so that they involve the readers and spark their imaginations.

Yet we don't have to use complex ideas or eloquent words to reach out to each other. I give you the gift of simple words that connect us on a soul-to-soul level. I make this powerful connection by allowing God to inspire me in what I say to you. My simple words are heartfelt and true.

Based upon my own experiences, I know that even a few words can deliver a mighty message. When I affirm: *God is love* or *God is with us*, I feel infused with strength by these simple messages of truth, and I pray you feel that strength as well.

Even though these words may not be original to me or to you, they speak to our hearts and serve as a reminder that simple words can be powerfully inspiring and profound.

> **"The words that I have spoken to you
> are spirit and life."**—John 6:63

Day 286

---◆---

God, we welcome You as our guide to
a richer, more fulfilling life.

WELCOME!

Whenever we are inviting people into our home, we welcome them with sincere, warmhearted expressions of our acceptance of them. We welcome family and friends into a peaceful atmosphere of love and congeniality that we help create and maintain.

We also welcome opportunities to bring our awareness of God into our own life experiences. Because we are receptive to learning more from God and to spending more time in prayer with God, we enrich every aspect of our life.

We welcome God into our thoughts, knowing that God is always with us. Our invitation to God reminds us to be open to our Creator as our guide to a richer, more fulfilling life.

> **"Welcome one another, therefore, just as Christ**
> **has welcomed you, for the glory of God."**
> **—Romans 15:7**

Day 287

♦

God assures us that we
are complete and whole.

COMPLETE AND WHOLE
Something may have happened to us physically or emotionally that left us feeling less than complete and whole. Yet we meet any seemingly life-altering experiences with resilience when we remember that our wholeness is made up of mind, body, and spirit.

We are more than physical beings who are able to reason. God's spirit lives within us as an eternal presence of life that makes us complete. Even though God's spirit enlivens us, it is up to us to accept the truth of our spiritual nature and to draw upon the power and understanding it provides.

All our thoughts, words, and actions are from our awareness of God. We are one with the love, peace, and power of the universe. God assures us that we are complete and whole.

> "The eye is the lamp of the body. So, if your eye
> is healthy, your whole body will be full of light."
> —Matthew 6:22

Day 288

—◆—

Prayer is a sacred practice that keeps us attuned to God and the blessings of God.

PRAYING

Practice does help us perfect our skills and talents. However, we don't have to be trying for perfection to know that the positiveness we apply in our everyday living brings about beneficial results.

Having established good work, eating, and exercise practices, we feel good about what we are doing and feel better for doing it. We realize the benefits of putting ideas about health of mind and body into practice.

And the single most important practice in our day, on any day, is prayer. We pray often, applying spiritual principles in both ordinary and extraordinary circumstances. This sacred practice keeps us attuned to God and the blessings of God.

"He was praying in a certain place, and after he
had finished, one of his disciples said to him,
'Lord, teach us to pray, as John taught his disciples.'"
—Luke 11:1

Day 289

---◆---

We are dedicated to expressing the qualities
of our sacred identity.

SACRED IDENTITY

Our faces, our names, and even our voices help identify us. Yet there is so much more to us than what can be seen and heard. We have a spiritual identity that lives out through our physical identity. We are both sacred and human.

Although the human identity may change over the years, our spiritual identity is ageless and eternal. The spirit of God is at the core of our being, and knowing that sacred qualities are inherent to us adds meaning and purpose to our life every day.

Our true selves are loving and wise, understanding and compassionate. We know we are being true to our spiritual selves and to God when we live from the sacred qualities of God's spirit within us.

> **"You are the light of the world."**
> **—Matthew 5:14**

Day 290

All life is worthy of our honor.

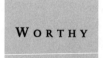
WORTHY

Watching a tiny spider weave silken thread into an intricate, delicate web, we are in awe of God's creativity. God created the spider and imprinted the complex pattern for the web within it.

Every day, we want to recognize and value the creativity of God in all life. Every person we meet today is a creation of great worth. Every animal is a design of divine intention. On land, in the air, and in streams and oceans, all of nature is teeming with life.

We do all that we know to do to support the excellence that God has created. We honor God in praise and by knowing that we, too, have value. We are worthy of God's blessings, and we accept them gratefully.

"Finally, beloved, whatever is true, whatever is honorable,
whatever is just . . . whatever is commendable,
if there is any excellence and if there is anything worthy
of praise, think about these things."
—Philippians 4:8

DAILY WORD FOR COUPLES

Day 291

God is the answer to our every prayer.

ANSWERED PRAYER Children may believe that they can be satisfied and fulfilled only if they receive exactly what they want, when they want it. Parents realize that instant gratification is only temporary and leads to disappointment.

We may have given specific prayer requests to God and then been surprised when the outcome was even better than we had anticipated it would be. What we have learned is that God knows what is best for us in every situation.

So rather than asking for or expecting a specific outcome, we rely on God's wisdom and judgment. God knows what is best concerning our relationship, our careers, and our finances. In all matters of our life and in all that matters in life, God is the answer. God is the answer to our every prayer.

> "Your Father knows what you need
> before you ask him."
> —Matthew 6:8

Day 292

◆

God is first in every choice we make.

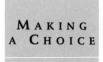

MAKING A CHOICE Knowing that we have choices seems like a luxury. Thinking that we have to make a choice may seem like work.

Life is full of choices, and we make some without any conscious consideration. We appreciate that we can agree on a favorite restaurant or television show. When our choices differ on these and other matters, however, we may have difficulty settling on which choice is the final one.

The choices we make impact our life and our relationship. So we ask God to help us decide what to choose. By making God the starting point in considering our choices, we are applying divine wisdom in every choice we make.

"There was a leper who came to him and knelt before him, saying, 'Lord, if you choose, you can make me clean.' He stretched out his hand and touched him, saying, 'I do choose. Be made clean!' Immediately his leprosy was cleansed."
—Matthew 8:2–3

DAILY WORD FOR COUPLES

Day 293

—◆—

Wherever we go, however we travel,
we are in God's care and keeping.

SAFE TRAVEL

Whether we are traveling on a long journey or taking a short commute to work, we affirm that we are in God's care and keeping.

Before we board an airplane, train, bus, ship—whatever form of transportation we may take—we pause for a moment to bless the people who have responsibilities on the journey. Thankful that these skilled men and women are dedicated to doing their best, we envision them giving their time and attention to every detail of their work.

To others, the journey we experience as passengers may seem to be in someone else's hands. In reality, we are in God's care and keeping, where we are safe and secure. Wherever we are going, and however we are getting there, God is taking care of us.

> "The Lord went in front of them in a pillar
> of cloud by day, to lead them along the way,
> and in a pillar of fire by night, to give them light,
> so that they might travel by day and by night."
> —Exodus 13:21

Day 294

---◆---

Letting go and letting God, we are preparing ourselves for accomplishments.

ACCOMPLISH-MENTS By thinking that we have to be in control of a situation, we may be thinking ourselves into a dilemma. We rescue ourselves by acknowledging that our quest in life is not about being in control; it's about letting God express life, love, and understanding through us.

Rather than trying to impose our will, we let go and let God. We are simply recognizing that God is actively at work in our lives. When we let go and let God do what God does best, we are relieving ourselves of stress. God knows better than we do, so we do let go.

God cares for us and about us, and God's love fills us with strength of mind and heart. There is so much we can accomplish by letting go of worry and letting God bring about divine results.

"Teach me your way, O Lord,
that I may walk in your truth;
give me an undivided heart to revere your name."
—Psalms 86:11

Day 295

———◆———

*Now is the time for setting
new goals and priorities.*

Until Now

Circumstances may have caused us to alter plans concerning our work or our personal life. Yet we view a change of plans as an opportunity for us to exercise our capacity for discovering more of what we are able to achieve.

Until now we may not have had an occasion that called on us to live up to our full creative potential. Until now we may have felt as though we have settled for less than we thought we were worthy of because we seemed to have found a familiar niche in life.

Now we reevaluate our priorities and set new goals for ourselves. With God strengthening us and revealing our potential to us, we move forward with confidence.

> "He sustained him in a desert land,
> in a howling wilderness waste;
> he shielded him, cared for him,
> guarded him as the apple of his eye."
> —Deuteronomy 32:10

Day 296

— ◆ —

*By accepting God into our life, we are
also accepting God's blessings.*

ACCEPTANCE

Our faith in God is the key to accepting ourselves for who we are and our world for what it is. Acceptance is an act of faith. Because we accept God as the answer to all that we need, we will find answers to every question.

We no longer believe in mere appearances, for we know that the beautiful mystery of God is something beyond human sight, sound, and understanding. We may never know exactly how or why God works in our life, but the beautiful part is that we do not need to know. We simply need to accept that God is actively at work in us and through us.

Because we have accepted God into our life, we accept the joy, peace, and love that God continually offers us. Accepting the sacred into our life blesses us.

> "As a deer longs for flowing streams,
> so my soul longs for you, O God.
> My soul thirsts for God."
> —Psalms 42:1–2

Day 297

As God's creations, we are within a circle
of ever-renewing life.

CIRCLE OF LIFE

Droplets of rainwater on surfaces seem to disappear soon after the sun comes out. However, those droplets do not cease to exist. They change form and are dissipated into the air. As vapor, they are carried along in the atmosphere.

Perhaps they will be caught up in light and reflect the colors of a rainbow. Eventually they will reappear, falling to earth again to nourish a beautiful rose or become a part of a stream or freshen the air.

We believe that all God's creations are held within a divine circle—a circle in which life never ends but does change form and becomes a part of something greater. We give thanks that we are part of this circle of life.

We do believe in God's power and wisdom. God's glory is far greater than we could ever envision, and we are thankful to be within the circle of God's ever-renewing life.

"Lord, I believe."
—John 9:38

Day 298

God satisfies the longing of our souls.

SATISFIED SOUL   Oh, it is so pure and unmistakable— the satisfaction we feel within our souls. As we immerse our whole beings in the presence of God, there is no thought other than the thought of God. There is no sound, but a message of assurance reaches beyond our senses: We are loved and cherished by our Creator.

God never disappoints us when we turn within in a time of silence. We move beyond the point of having to think about solving anything into a realm of knowing that God will provide the solution. We listen and learn from God.

God does fulfill our every desire and inspires us to live our lives from the fullness of our satisfied souls. We know and express that fullness as joy.

> "Let us approach with a true heart
> in full assurance of faith,
> with our hearts sprinkled clean."
> —Hebrews 10:22

Day 299

———◆———

Our Prayer

Dear God,

We know that the greatest strength is not limited to the physical realm. Neither is the most stalwart courage built up by the reasoning mind. The mighty strength of a spiritual being and the resolute courage of an overcomer reside within us.

Even though we may feel as if we are in a vulnerable position or condition, we have the strength and courage of Your spirit within us. Your pervading presence is our sanctuary of peace and order wherever we are, wherever we go.

You are with us as we prepare to lie down in our bed at home or in a bed during a stop in our travels away from home. You are with us as we walk, drive, or ride to each destination, whether we are in familiar or unfamiliar territory.

Thank You, God, for strength and courage!

"God is with you wherever you go."
—Joshua 1:9

Day 300

—◆—

My Gift to You

> **I GIVE YOU THE GIFT OF MY RENEWED COMMITMENT TO YOU AND OUR RELATIONSHIP.**

We began our life together with a commitment to love each other. That commitment helped us in times of uncertainty and challenge. Yet it was our commitment to acknowledging God's presence in each other and every situation we faced that truly brought us through it all.

So today I give you the gift of my renewed commitment. With this commitment, I truly see God's presence shining from you, I actually hear the wonder of divine ideas being expressed by you, and I gratefully feel the love that passes between us in our conversations and in our quiet moments.

You have greatly enriched my life, and it is my pleasure to give you the gift of a commitment that renews itself through the love of God that we share every day.

"Beloved, let us love one another, because love
is from God; everyone who loves is born
of God and knows God."
—1 John 4:7

BEING AWARE OF EACH OTHER

BY DIXIE CARTER

Both my husband, Hal Holbrook, and I continue to look for and discover the best in each other. We try to maximize our awareness of each other's best qualities and minimize the things that might drive each other nuts.

Hal appreciates that I have creative ideas and enthusiasm. On the other hand, I change my mind quite a lot, and this is hard on Hal, who is extremely orderly. Having attended military academies in his childhood, he was raised by the book, and he requires order in his life now. Even though I try to be respectful of his need for order, my rather impulsive nature makes it difficult. I race around trying to do a lot of things at one time. I'm inclined to jump first and then to review what I have done and try to fix it.

Hal is unpredictable in his own way. For instance, one night I was about to drift off to sleep and I heard *crunch, crunch*! Hal was sitting in the easy chair across the bedroom, eating an apple.

DAILY WORD FOR COUPLES

I sat up in bed and announced, "In all my life, I've never heard of anyone eating an apple at 11:30 at night!" The *crunch, crunch,* continued. "How can I sleep," I grumbled, "with all that noise?"

"Well, I do believe, Dixie, that you're as sensitive as the princess in the Princess and the Pea story. You hear a crunch from clear across the room that a normal person couldn't possibly hear." His humorous evaluation of my sensitivity took all the steam out of my indignation, and I couldn't help but laugh.

Sometimes I believe that what Hal loves most about me is that I am so loyal to my family. He appreciates having a wife who is a real family-type woman—especially since he grew up without a family. After being abandoned by their mother and father, Hal and his little sisters were raised by their grandfather. Hal had a nanny and was sent to the finest of schools, but he didn't have the security that a mother and father provide.

I grew up in a big, loving family, and Hal is a member of that family now. He has my two daughters and my father, my sisters and my brother, and a bunch of other kinfolk. Hal has been accepted into this family circle with great love and enthusiasm.

There is so much to love about Hal. He is physically so beautiful and quite fastidious. One of the things I so appreciate is that Hal is a perfect gentleman. When we met while making a movie for television, Hal was already an established actor, and I was a single mom just getting started. Yet it was Hal's great pleasure to give me—not just center stage—but the entire stage wherever we were. When people would approach us, asking for *his* autograph, he would say, "You'd better be asking Dixie for her autograph, 'cause one of these days, you're going to be mighty glad that you've got it."

Hal had been baptized as a child but was not active in any religion when we met. Throughout my life, I had been a churchgoer. After Hal got to know me better, he asked if I really liked going to church so much or was I just going to take my two daughters. I told him the truth: I felt better when I went to church. I needed to be nourished spiritually and going to church made me happy.

Then one day a few months later, he said, "Could I go with you sometime?"

"I'd love for you to go with us!" My heart was beating pretty fast, I confess, for I had hoped that he would go with my daughters and me. Sure enough he did—partly because he loved me and wanted to go where I was going, and partly for other things that we, quite frankly, don't talk about. Sometimes one's own religious convictions defy explanation, and I just allow his to be private.

My family had a formal upbringing in terms of religion. We prayed in church, we prayed alone, and we prayed at the table together. Hal and I continue that tradition.

My work on a television series keeps me close to

DAILY WORD FOR COUPLES

home, but Hal has done a couple of independent movies. When he is on location, we miss each other. Absence, in our case, does make the heart grow even fonder. We have a good time together, and when we are apart, we can't wait to get back with each other.

There are some simple things that help make being together enjoyable. Listening to what each other is saying is important. When we really listen, we understand each other. We explain what we like and don't like. Sometimes, it's just as simple as one of us letting the other know, "I don't want to talk at the breakfast table this morning. Let me have my coffee, and then we can talk." Then the other will say, "I can't stand to have you not greet me in the morning, so could you please just give me a hug and a kiss to start my day off nicely." Simple things create the beginning of an orderly day.

Something as simple as helping each other make the bed in the morning allows a sweetness to pass between two people who are sharing a task. Both have to be willing to ask for help and to help. Sometimes I forget to ask. For instance, when Hal and I are enjoying a quiet winter evening at our home in Tennessee, I may wish that he would notice that the fire is about to go out instead of my asking him to put another log in the fireplace. Instead of asking, I watch the fire die down to a burning ember and then grumble and huff and puff as I go out in the snow to get a log. That's just ridiculous, but it's very human.

I have, however, come to an important realization over the years: By denying myself the little pleasure of being angry and hanging on to grudges, I am a happier person and I share that happiness with Hal.

I have also learned that when a situation begins to get edgy in a marriage, it's wonderful to have loving family to turn to. Sitting at the kitchen table with a cup of coffee and with family who are the best friends you have in the world can bring out the best in a marriage.

One night several years ago, Hal had locked my daughter Ginna out of the house on her first night of solo driving. He was usually the last one up at night, so he always closed up at night—locking the doors and turning out the lights—before going to bed. When Ginna came home, she was so frightened about being locked out that she was trembling. Within a few minutes, Ginna was okay and had gone to bed. Hal had gone to bed, but I was sitting in our dining room in the dark, sulking. I couldn't understand how Hal had forgotten that Ginna was not home yet.

A little later, Daddy, who was there on a visit, came down to the kitchen to graze, as he calls it, at the refrigerator and sensed that someone was there in the dark. Then barefooted and in his pajamas, Daddy sat down

DAILY WORD FOR COUPLES

and made the sweetest speech: He reminded me how much Hal loved me and how much he loved my daughters. "Dixie," he said, "Hal is a rare man, a kind and good man. He has been a good father to Ginna and Mary." Daddy did not tell me anything I did not already know, but hearing it from someone I loved and trusted so much made the difference. I wasn't a bit angry by the time I left the dining room that night.

What does a couple do that doesn't have other family to help them move beyond an impasse in their relationship? They can look to friends who really love them and have their best interests at heart. It only takes a few deep friendships to sustain an individual or a couple.

For most couples, making up their minds to hold on to their marriage is crucial to making it work. Going to church together, going to the preacher or to a family therapist and talking through problems help. The two individuals in a marriage chose each other for some good reasons and continuing to concentrate on those reasons and searching out new ones bless the union. These are things that we can do before we call it quits and walk away.

I love the wisdom of advice my grandmother often gave: A good marriage consists of two bears: *bear* and *forbear*. I believe that a couple that does bear and forbear *together* are richly rewarded.

ABOUT THE
FEATURED AUTHORS

Steve Allen, who passed away in October 2000, was a popular TV comedian from the Golden Age of Comedy of the 1950s. An award-winning actor and writer, he has starred in several motion pictures and television shows, including the *Tonight* show, which he created and hosted, and *The Steve Allen Comedy Hour.* Steve was inducted into the TV Academy's Hall of Fame, wrote over 8,000 songs, made over 50 record albums and CDs, and authored 53 books.

Troylyn Ball is a devoted wife and mother. Her son Marshall Stewart Ball was born with a host of disabilities, including the inability to walk or speak. With the love and devotion of Troylyn and her husband, Charlie, Marshall learned to write by pointing to individual letters on an alphabet board. He has completed hundreds of writings and his book *Kiss of God* has sold hundreds of thousands of copies. He has been featured on *Oprah*, *CNN/Time*, and in *People* magazine.

Dorothy Bridges was a career wife for 60 years and is mother to the Lloyd Bridges family, which includes Jeff, Beau, and Lucinda. She has 11 grandchildren. Dorothy's poems and articles have appeared in various magazines and she recently coauthored *From Timber Ridge to Daymer Gardens: A Journey in Words* with Thorsten Kaye. Her latest projects include a children's book and a collection of love poems. A native of Los Angeles, Dorothy lives in the same house where she and Lloyd raised their family—one block from the UCLA campus where they met over 60 years ago.

Dixie Carter is probably best known for her role as Julia Sugarbaker on the hit TV series *Designing Women*. An award-winning actress, singer, and author, she currently appears on the television show *Family Law* and has a recurring role on *Ladies Man*. Dixie has made numerous appearances on stage and screen, appeared in two yoga videos, recorded two music CDs, and authored *Trying to Get to Heaven: Opinions of a Tennessee Talker*. Dixie has two daughters, Ginna and Mary Dixie Carter, and is married to actor Hal Holbrook.

Roger Crawford was born with the birth defect ectro-dactyly, but went on to compete in tennis, earning two varsity letters at Loyola Marymount University. He was the first disabled athlete to compete in a NCAA Division I sport. Roger currently holds professional certification from the U.S. Professional Tennis Association. Now an award-winning and sought-after speaker, he is the author of *Playing from the Heart* and *How High Can You Bounce?*

Delilah is a full-time wife and mother and also a syndi-cated nighttime DJ who weaves telephone calls with a blend of love songs and ballads. Heard nightly in 195 markets, Delilah has the highest-rated, fastest-growing syndicated show in the history of adult contemporary radio. She and her husband, Doug, reside in Seattle with their children: Sonny, Shaylah, Emmanuelle, Zachariah, and two foster children.

"Jungle" Jack Hanna, popular host of the hit television series, *Jack Hanna's Animal Adventures*, is one of America's most beloved naturalists and adventurers. He is director

emeritus of the Columbus Zoo in Columbus, Ohio, and is a regular guest on television shows such as *Good Morning America*, *The Late Show with David Letterman*, *Live with Regis*, and *The Maury Povich Show*. An author and sought-after speaker, Jack makes countless personal appearances throughout the United States and is an active supporter of Easter Seals and the Leukemia Society.

Jayne Meadows-Allen is an Emmy-award winner and five-time Emmy nominee. She is an accomplished actress of stage, screen, and television. Jayne has received many honors, including the American Book Award and the International Platform Association Award for her one-woman show, *Powerful Women in History*. She is an active member of an entertainment industry that includes her son, producer Bill Allen.

Dave Pelzer was identified as one of the most severely abused children in California's history. As a young adult Dave was determined to better himself—no matter what the odds. A highly sought-after speaker, Dave is author of the *New York Times* Best Sellers *A Child Called "It," The Lost Boy*, and *A Man Named Dave*. He recently released a new book entitled *Help Yourself*. Dave has received the prestigious J.C. Penney Golden Rule Award and named one of the Ten Outstanding Young Americans. He was the only American to be honored as The Outstanding Young Persons of the World in 1994. Dave's incredible life's story has been featured on *The Montel Williams Show*, *The Sally Jesse Raphael Show*, and *The View*.

Gracie Rosenberger toured with the Continental Singers throughout North America, Europe, and the Middle East for two seasons as a featured soloist prior to her car accident.

ABOUT THE FEATURED AUTHORS

Since her recovery, she has recorded a music CD and has been nominated to the Board of Directors for the Amputee Coalition of America as well as the Limbs for Life Foundation. Gracie has numerous television and live appearances to her credit. Gracie, her husband, Peter, and sons, Parker and Grayson, reside in Nashville. She continues to focus on the future with goals of rappelling, in-line skating, writing a book, and being a "little-league mom." Gracie and Peter's Web site, www.gracieandpeter.com, draws a large audience from around the world.

Peter Rosenberger was a music major at Belmont University in Nashville, where he met his future wife, Gracie. Together they travel across the United States speaking and performing before churches, organizations, and universities and have appeared on various television shows. In addition to public appearances with Gracie, Peter has worked for two administrations in Tennessee state government and is actively involved in the leadership of such fields as management training, health care, and human resources.

ABOUT THE FEATURED AUTHORS

ABOUT THE
DAILY WORD EDITORS

The *Daily Word* editors have coauthored and coedited *Daily Word: Love, Inspiration, and Guidance for Everyone*; *Daily Word Prayer Journal*; *Daily Word for Women*; *Daily Word for Families*; and *Daily Word for Healing*.

Elaine Meyer has served in the Silent Unity ministry of Unity School of Christianity since 1987 and is the assistant editor of *Daily Word* magazine. She is also a published poet and writer. Elaine, her husband, Dale, and their daughter, Caitlin, reside in rural Missouri.

Janie Wright served as associate editor of *Daily Word* magazine for 12 years. Janie lives with her daughter, Natalie, in the greater Kansas City, Missouri, area.

Colleen Zuck has been editor of *Daily Word* magazine since 1985. She also served as editor of *Wee Wisdom*, the longest continuously published magazine for children in the United States. She lives with her husband, Bill, in rural Missouri.